D1526665

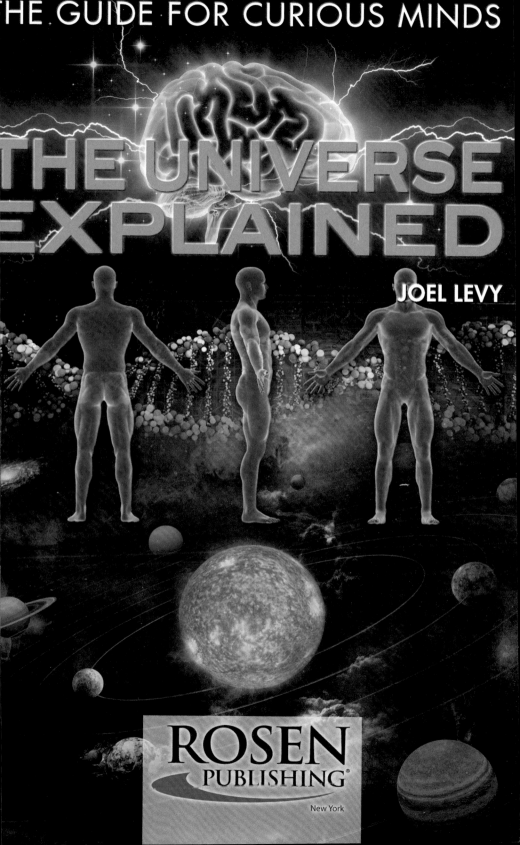

THE GUIDE FOR CURIOUS MINDS

THE UNIVERSE EXPLAINED

JOEL LEVY

ROSEN
PUBLISHING®

New York

This edition published in 2014 by:

The Rosen Publishing Group, Inc.
29 East 21st Street
New York, NY 10010

Additional end matter copyright © 2014 by The Rosen Publishing Group, Inc.

Library of Congress Cataloging-in-Publication Data

Levy, Joel.
The Universe explained/Joel Levy.—First edition.
    pages cm.—(The guide for curious minds)
Audience: Grade 7 to 12.
Includes bibliographical references and index.
ISBN 978-1-4777-2958-8 (library bound)
1. Science—Miscellanea—Juvenile literature. 2. Astronomy—Miscellanea—juvenile literature. 3. Handbooks, vade-mecums, etc.—Juvenile literature I. Title.
Q163.L44 2014
500—dc23

                                                                    2013029636

Manufactured in the United States of America

CPSIA Compliance Information: Batch #W14YA: For further information, contact Rosen Publishing, New York, New York, at 1-800-237-9932.

© 2014 ELWIN STREET PRODUCTIONS
Elwin Street Productions
3 Percy Street
London W1, UK
www.elwinstreet.com

Metric Conversion Chart

1 inch = 2.54 centimeters
1 foot = 30.48 centimeters
1 yard = .914 meters
1 square foot = .093 square meters
1 square mile = 2.59 square kilometers
1 ton = .907 metric tons
1 pound = 454 grams
1 mile = 1.609 kilometers

1 cup = 250 milliliters
1 ounce = 28 grams
1 fluid ounce = 30 milliliters
1 teaspoon = 5 milliliters
1 tablespoon = 15 milliliters
355 degrees F = 180 degrees Celsius

89 THE HUMAN BODY

103 HUMAN ENDEAVOR

117 GENERAL REFERENCE

THE
UNIVERSE

Astronomers estimate the age of the universe in two different ways. One way is by determining the age of the oldest stars; the other is by measuring the density of the universe and using that to extrapolate its rate of expansion, and therefore its age. The oldest-known stars are found in globular clusters—dense swarms of stars of the same age—and are estimated to be between 11 and 18 billion years old. The second method gives an age range of between 11.5 and 14.5 billion years. Overall, the consensus is that the universe is around some 13 billion years old.

How Big is the Universe?

The size of the universe depends on its density and whether it will continue to expand, remain stable, or collapse. If it keeps on expanding, the universe is infinitely large. If it remains stable or collapses, the universe could be up to 100 billion light years. Given the tremendous scale involved, special units of distance are used when measuring the universe (see the table below).

Name of unit	Derivation of unit	Distance
Astronomical unit	Average distance between Earth and Sun	~93 million miles (149.7 million km)
Light year	Distance traveled by light in one year	5,865,696,000,000 miles (9.4 trillion km)
Light second	Distance traveled by light in one second	186,000 miles (299,338 km)
Light nanosecond	Distance traveled by light in one-billionth of a second	1 foot (30.5 cm)
Parsec	Parallax second of arc (*)	3,258 light years (19,110,437,568,000 miles); 30.8 trillion km
Megaparsec	1 million parsecs	3,258,000 light years (~20 million trillion miles); 32 million trillion km

(*) Parallax is the phenomenon where stationary objects at different distances from a moving observer appear to move relative to one another (e.g. to a train passenger, the foreground appears to move relative to the background). Apparent movement of stars in the night sky, such as is caused by a parallax, is measured in terms of degrees of arc. A second is a sixtieth of a minute, which is a sixtieth of a degree.

The "Big Bang"

The current theory says that the universe was extremely tiny and extremely hot in the beginning, but that it underwent radical expansion to form the universe we know today. The table below gives a countdown to the "Big Bang" and the chief events in the subsequent development of the universe.

Time after "beginning" of universe	Major events	Description
10^{-43} seconds	Planck era and inflationary era	Time and space don't exist in the usual sense; there is neither matter nor radiation
10^{-12}–10^{-10} seconds	Radiation fills the universe	The "Big Bang" as we understand it begins. Universe coalesces into very high-energy soup of radiation
10^{-4} seconds	Matter comes into being	Protons and neutrons, the building blocks of matter, are formed
100 seconds	Nucleosynthesis	Protons and neutrons form nuclei of lightest elements—hydrogen, helium, and lithium
500,000 years	Formation of first atoms	Nuclei capture electrons, forming first atoms—hydrogen, helium, and lithium
1 billion years	Formation of stars	Gravity causes balls of gas to coalesce. These grow until they collapse under their own weight, triggering fusion and igniting the first stars
2 billion years–present day	Formation of the universe as we know it	Fusion creates heavier elements. Planets form and life evolves
What next?	The end of the universe?	The universe continues expanding and cooling forever. Eventually, stars burn up all their fuel and the universe grows cold

The Oldest Light in the Universe

A NASA satellite captured the sharpest-ever picture of the afterglow of the Big Bang in February 2003. Scientists used NASA's Wilkinson Microwave Anistropy Probe (WMAP) to capture this new cosmic portrait.

This light emerged 380,000 years after the Big Bang. The light we see today, known as the cosmic microwave background, has traveled over 13 billion years to reach us. Within this light are infinitesimal patterns that mark the seeds of what later grew into clusters of galaxies. These patterns are tiny temperature differences within this extraordinarily evenly dispersed microwave light bathing the universe, which now averages a frigid 2.73 degrees above absolute zero temperature.

The new portrait precisely pegged the age of the universe at 13.7 billion years, with a small one percent margin of error. The data revealed that the first generation of stars to shine in the universe first ignited only 200 million years after the Big Bang, much earlier than standard models suggest.

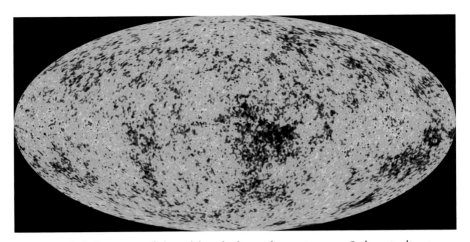

ABOVE A full-sky map of the oldest light in the universe. Colors indicate "warmer" (red) and "cooler" (blue) spots.

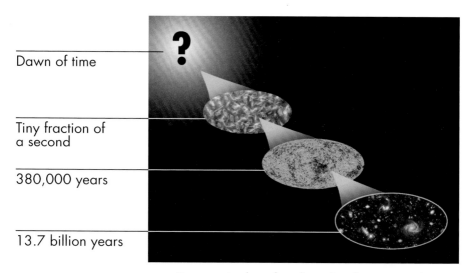

Dawn of time

Tiny fraction of
a second

380,000 years

13.7 billion years

ABOVE Patterns in the afterglow develop into galaxies.

Exoplanets

Exoplanets are planets that are orbiting stars outside of our own Solar System. The first such planet, 51 Pegasi A, was discovered in 1995 by a Swiss team led by Michel Mayor and Didier Queloz. Since then, over 150 exoplanets have been detected.

The oldest-known exoplanet orbits a binary star in the M4 globular cluster in the constellation Scorpius (5,600 light years away) and could be 13 billion years old.

The planet with the shortest orbital period found so far is Ogle-TR-3 A, a Jupiter-like planet that orbits its sun in just 28 hours and 33 minutes. Another Jupiter-like planet that orbits close to its sun is HD209458 B (150 light years away); observations by the Hubble Telescope show that its hydrogen atmosphere is being evaporated at a rate of 10,000 tons/second.

The most distant exoplanet is the above-mentioned planet in the M4 globular cluster, 5,600 light years away. Epsilon Eridani C, which is one-tenth as massive as Jupiter and 10 light years away, is the closest and smallest exoplanet yet detected.

Galaxies

Spiral galaxies (of which ours is one): *arms loop out from globular or bar-shaped central hub. Sub-categorized into "edge-on" or "face-on" spiral galaxies (depending on their orientation to Earth) or Seyfert galaxies, if especially bright.*

Elliptical galaxies: *no arms; "squashed" or spherical shape.*
Irregular galaxies: *no distinct shape.*
Radiogalaxies: *very hot galaxies emitting radio and thermal radiation.*
Quasars: *thought to be visual echoes of very young galactic centers.*

The nearest spiral galaxy to our own is Andromeda. At 2.2 million light years away, it is the most distant object that can be seen with the naked eye. Furthermore, it is the only object outside of our own galaxy that can be seen with the naked eye.

The nearest invisible galaxy to our own is the Sagittarius dwarf galaxy, 100,000 light years away. The nearest visible galaxy is the Large Magellanic Cloud, 169,000 light years away.

All of these galactic neighbors and our Milky Way are members of the so-called Local Group, which is hurtling at 375 miles (603.5 km)/second toward the Virgo Cluster, some 45 million light years away.

The Milky Way

Our own galaxy is a spiral galaxy that revolves around a point known as galactic central. The latter is probably home to a huge black hole a million times heavier than the Sun—not that anyone can know for sure, since the massive gravity field inside a black hole means that not even light can escape.

The "hub" of the Milky Way is a bulge consisting of hundreds of millions of stars. Our Solar System sits near the edge of one of the thin arms that spiral outward from the hub. This arm is called the Orion Arm, because it contains the bright stars from the constellation Orion.

Number of stars in Milky Way: *approx. 200–700 billion.*
Span: *100,000 light years.*
Thickness: *~2,000–5,000 light years.*
**Speed of Milky Way's movement toward center of Local
Group:** *25 miles (40 km)/second.*

Closest Stars

The closest star to our Solar System is actually a system of three stars, called the Alpha Centauri System. It consists of Alpha Centauri, Rigil Kentaurus, and Proxima Centauri. Proxima Centauri is slightly closer to us than are her two sisters—the star is 4.22 light years from Earth (24.8 trillion miles; 39.9 trillion km). Alpha Centauri is 4.35 light years from Earth (25.6 trillion miles; 41.2 trillion km). The Sun is the closest star to Earth.

Life Cycle of a Star

All stars are born from stellar nebulae—stellar nurseries consisting of enormous clouds of gas, areas of which collapse into huge balls, which may then ignite into stars. In other words, every star in the universe starts out the same way.

What happens to the star through the rest of its life depends on the precise size of this initial ball of gas. If the ball of gas is too small, it will not ignite at all, and instead will become a brown giant (essentially a very large version of Jupiter). If it is of an "average" size, it will follow a life cycle akin to that of our own Sun. If it is "massive," it may eventually become a black hole.

FACT! The star HD70642 (95 light years away) has the most similar planetary system to our own—it has a Jupiter-like world that orbits it once every six years (as opposed to Jupiter's 12 years). This raises the possibility that it may have Earth-like planets orbiting it at a distance favorable to the evolution of life.

Constellations

Constellations are imaginary patterns drawn between stars in the night sky. We know that some of the same constellations we see today were visible to Ice Age humans, because prehistoric star maps have been found painted on cave walls and preserved on bone and rock. Nonetheless, the majority of our constellations' names today come from the Ancient Greeks.

In 1922, the International Astronomical Union (IAU) standardized the names and forms of 88 major constellations, shown on the star maps on these pages.

Northern sky

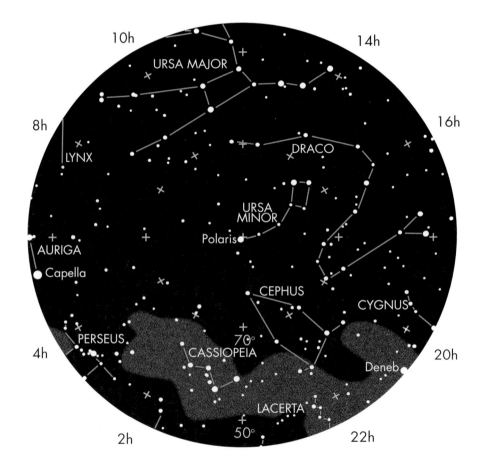

Locating the constellations takes practice and a star map. The easiest way is to use a familiar star or constellation as a reference. The best-known reference points are the Big Dipper (Plough) grouping of stars in the Northern Hemisphere, and the Southern Cross in the Southern Hemisphere. The shading represents the position of the Milky Way.

In the Northern Hemisphere, the Pole Star is in the center. To find it in the night sky, first locate the Great Bear (Ursa Major), and trace the Pole Star by means of its "pointers."

Southern sky

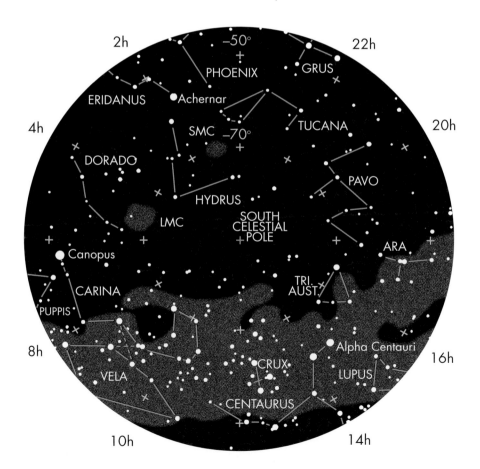

The 88 constellations are given here with the hemisphere in which they are primarily visible (North or South). Constellations become higher or lower in the sky with the changing of the seasons. Thus many of them will be visible in different hemispheres at different

Constellation	Common name	Hemisphere most visible	Constellation	Common name	Hemisphere most visible
Andromeda	Daughter of Cassiopeia	N	Circinus	The Compasses	S
Antlia	The Air Pump	S	Columba	The Dove	S
Apus	Bird of Paradise	S	Coma Berenices	Berenice's Hair	N
Aquarius	The Water Bearer	N/S	Corona Australis	The Southern Crown	S
Aquila	The Eagle	N/S	Corona Borealis	The Northern Crown	N
Ara	The Altar	S			
Aries	The Ram	N/S	Corvus	The Crow	N/S
Auriga	The Charioteer	N	Crater	The Cup	N/S
Bootes	The Herdsman	N	Crux	The Southern Cross	S
Caelum	The Chisel	S	Cygnus	The Swan	N
Camelo-pardus	The Giraffe	N	Delphinus	The Dolphin	N/S
Cancer	The Crab	N/S	Dorado	The Goldfish	S
Canes Venatici	The Hunting Dogs	N	Draco	The Dragon	N
			Equuleus	The Little Horse	N/S
Canis Major	The Big Dog	N/S	Eridanus	The River	N/S
Canis Minor	The Little Dog	N/S	Fornax	The Furnace	S
Capricornus	The Horned Goat	N/S	Gemini	The Twins	N/S
Carina	The Keel of the Argo	S	Grus	The Crane	S
Cassiopeia	The Queen	N	Hercules	The Son of Zeus	N
Centaurus	The Centaur	N/S	Horologium	The Clock	S
Cepheus	The King	N	Hydra	The Water Snake	N/S
Cetus	The Whale	N/S	Hydrus	The Little Water Snake	S
Chamaeleon	The Chamaeleon	S			

times of the year, while some will be visible to both hemispheres for much of the time.

Where a star is visible in both hemispheres for significant parts of the year, it is marked N/S on this chart.

Constellation	Common name	Hemisphere most visible	Constellation	Common name	Hemisphere most visible
Indus	The Indian	S	Pisces Australis	The Southern Fish	S
Lacerta	The Lizard	N	Puppis	The Stern of the Argo	S
Leo	The Lion	N/S	Pyxis	The Compass	S
Leo Minor	The Little Lion	N	Reticulum	The Reticle	S
Lepus	The Hare	S	Sagitta	The Arrow	N
Libra	The Balance	N/S	Sagittarius	The Archer	N/S
Lupus	The Wolf	N/S	Scorpius	The Scorpion	N/S
Lynx	The Lynx	N	Sculptor	The Sculptor	S
Lyra	The Harp	N	Scutum	The Shield	N/S
Mensa	Table Mountain	S	Serpens	The Serpent	N/S
Micro-scopium	The Microscope	S	Sextans	The Sextant	N/S
Monoceros	The Unicorn	N/S	Taurus	The Bull	N/S
Musca	The Fly	S	Telescopium	The Telescope	S
Norma	The Square	S	Triangulum	The Triangle	N
Octans	The Octant	S	Triangulum Australis	The Southern Triangle	S
Ophiuchus	The Serpent Bearer	N/S	Tucana	The Toucan Bird	S
Orion	The Hunter	N/S	Ursa Major	The Great Bear	N
Pavo	The Peacock	S	Ursa Minor	The Little Bear	N
Pegasus	The Winged Horse	N	Vela	The Sails of the Argo	S
Perseus	Rescuer of Andromeda	N	Virgo	The Virgin	N/S
Phoenix	The Phoenix Bird	S	Volans	The Flying Fish	S
Pictor	The Painter	S	Vulpecula	The Fox	N
Pisces	The Fishes	N/S			

The Signs of the Zodiac

Even today many people confuse astronomy (the study of celestial bodies) with astrology (the study of celestial bodies with regard to their influence on human affairs). Until the 17th century, however, there was no such distinction. Several of the great figures of early astronomy who are now credited with transforming it from superstition to science—for example, Tycho Brahe and Johannes Kepler—owed their contemporary reputations and livelihoods to their work as astrologers.

The shapes we associate with the zodiacal constellations date back to the Babylonians (3rd millennium BCE*), and possibly further.

(*) BCE stands for Before the Common Era and is used in preference to BC (Before Christ). Nonetheless, it takes as its reference point the same "0" date—that is, the birth of Christ.

THE SOLAR SYSTEM

O ur Solar System is located in the Orion Arm, one of the outer spiral arms of the Milky Way galaxy, about 27,000 light years from the center. It is believed to have formed about 4.6 billion years ago, when a cloud of gas (mainly hydrogen) and dust coalesced into a huge ball surrounded by a flattened disc. The ball of gas at the center collapsed under its own weight, triggering fusion and becoming a star (the Sun), while slight perturbations in the disc caused areas of higher density to build up—these then began attracting more gas and dust and aggregating into planets.

Distance from Galactic Center: *27,000 light years (1.6 x 10^{17} miles).*
Speed of orbit around Galactic Center: *140 miles (225 km)/second.*
Time taken to complete one orbit around Galactic Center: *250 million years.*
Age: *4.6 billion years.*
Distance from Sun to most distant planet: *4.6 billion miles (7.4 billion km).*
Farthest-known object in Solar System (that is, orbiting the Sun): *1996 TL66 (a ball of ice and rock); distance from Sun is 12 billion miles (19.3 billion km).*
Maximum radius of Sun's influence (a.k.a. "heliopause"): *30 billion miles (48.3 billion km).*
Milestones in Solar System: *farthest planet is Pluto, 4.6 billion miles (7.4 billion km) from Sun; way beyond, at 12 billion miles (19.3 billion km), is the Kuiper belt (a ring of comets); the heliopause (limit of extent of solar particles) is 30 billion miles (48.3 billion km) away; the Oort Cloud (origin of long-period comets) is 6 trillion miles (9.7 trillion km) away.*

The Sun

The Sun is composed of a hot inner core, about 250,000 miles (402,336 km) across, and an outer, opaque layer, known as the convective zone, about 310,000 miles (498,897 km) thick. Heat is transferred from the inner core through the convective zone to the surface, or photosphere, which is only a few hundred miles thick. From here, light and heat radiate out through the transparent atmosphere, comprised of the chromosphere (a few thousand miles thick) and the corona. The corona can extend millions of miles out into space.

Age: *4.6 billion years.*
Spectral type: *G2V.*
Absolute magnitude: *4.8.*
Distance from Earth: *93 million miles (149.7 million km; 8 light minutes).*
Expected life span: *~10 billion years.*
Diameter: *863,354 miles (1.4 million km; = 109 Earth diameters).*
Mass: *1.989 x 10^{30} kg (= 99.8 percent of total mass of Solar System). 1,300,000 Earths could fit inside the Sun.*
Temperature: *11,120°F (6,160 degrees C) at surface; 28 million °F (15.5 million degrees C) at core.*
Core pressure: *250 billion atmospheres.*
Composition: *75 percent hydrogen; 25 percent helium; less than 0.1 percent other elements. Each second, the Sun converts 690,000,000 tonnes of hydrogen into 684,000,000 tonnes of helium—the difference is converted into energy. The photosphere, one of the outer layers where most of the light is given off, is 398,000 times brighter than the full Moon, and 1,000 times brighter than an equivalent-sized patch of clear sky on a sunny day.*

Sunspots

The markings—actually several thousand miles across—on the surface of the Sun are where the photosphere is cooler and darker. They are caused by intense, localized magnetic fields, although exactly how the latter can cause cooling is not properly understood.

The appearance of sunspots is linked to fluctuations in the Solar Wind (the stream of energetic particles that floods out from the Sun). These in turn affect the Earth's magnetosphere and ionosphere, and may even affect the climate. Very cold periods in Earth's history, such as the "Little Ice Age" of the late 17th century (when the Thames in London froze over several times), may be linked to periods of reduced sunspot activity on the Sun. Sunspot numbers increase and decrease in an 11-year cycle. The last peak was around 2012, making the next one due in 2023.

The Moon

In the past, some scientists believed that the Moon was formed from a rock that had split away from the Earth, leaving behind the depression that is the Pacific Basin. Others argued that it was a wandering planet that had been "captured" by Earth's gravity. Analysis of Moon rock now suggests that it was most likely formed when a planet the size of Mars struck the young Earth, propelling a huge jet of rock that then formed a ring around the Earth. Later, this coalesced to form the Moon as we know it.

Distance from Earth: *238,500 miles (383,829 km).*
Diameter: *2,159 miles (3,475 km).*
Mass: *7.35 x 10^{22} kg (10 billion trillion kg).*
Major features of the lunar surface as seen from Earth:
   light-colored highlands and mountain ridges; maria (dark lava plains).
Temperature variations on the surface: *−292°F to +239°F (-180 to 115 degrees C).*
Length of orbit: *the Moon orbits the Earth every 27.32 days.*
Order of phases of the Moon: *New Moon; waxing crescent; first quarter; waxing gibbous; Full Moon; waning gibbous; last quarter; waning crescent; New Moon.*

Comets

These are balls of ice, dust, and, occasionally, rock, which are normally confined to the very fringes of the Solar System, in the Oort Cloud. For reasons not yet fully understood, sometimes these balls become dislodged and begin to circle the Sun in highly elliptical and eccentric orbits. If one comes close enough to the Sun, the pressure of the Solar Wind causes particles of ice and rock to evaporate from the surface and stream out behind it in a glowing tail —giving the comet profile that we see from Earth.

Some comets have been observed a number of times through recorded history, so that their period—the length of time between visits to our part of the Solar System—is known. Others have been observed only once. Generally, comets are not named until they are re-observed, at which point they are named after their discoverers. See the chart below for a summary of the major comet discoveries.

Major comets	Discovered	Discoverer	Last (recorded) visit	Next visit	Period (years)
Halley	240 BCE	First sighted in antiquity	1986	2061	76
Biela	1772 CE	Wilhelm von Biela	1852	Broken up since	n.a.
Encke	1786	Johanne Encke	2013	2017	3.28
Faye	1843	Hervé-Auguste-Etienne-Albans Faye	2006	2014	7.34
Swift-Tuttle, a.k.a. Kegler (responsible for the Perseids meteor shower)	1862	Ernst Wilhelm Leberecht Tempel and Lewis Swift	1992	2126	About 130
Gehrels (78P)	1973	Tom Gehrels	2012	2019	5.5
Kohoutek	1973	Lubos Kohoutek	1973	76973	75,000
Howell (88P)	1981	Ellen Howell	2009	2015	5.5
Shoemaker-Levy 9	1993	Eugene and Carolyn Shoemaker and David Levy	1994	Impacted Jupiter	n.a.
Hale-Bopp	1995	Alan Hale and Thomas Bopp	1997	4385	2,520-2,533
Hyakutake	1996	Yuji Hyakutake	1996	31496	29,500
2001 Q4 (NEAT)	2001	NEAT comet search program	None	2004	Unknown
2002 T7 (LINEAR)	2002	LINEAR comet search program	None	2004	Unknown

The Planets

Imagine the Earth is the size of a grape, and the Moon is a foot (30.5 cm) away from it. The Sun would be a block away and about the height of a man, while Jupiter would be the size of a melon and about four blocks away. Saturn, another five blocks farther on, would be the size of an orange, while Uranus and Neptune, both the size of lemons, would be 20 and 30 blocks away from the Earth. The dwarf planet Pluto would be almost too small to see. You would be the size of an atom.

BELOW Orbital position of the planets in relation to the Sun

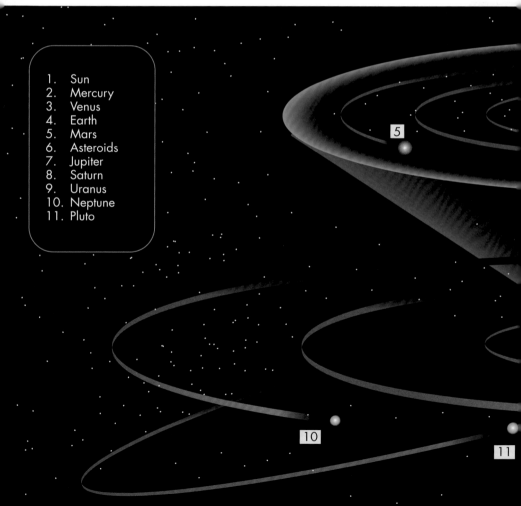

1. Sun
2. Mercury
3. Venus
4. Earth
5. Mars
6. Asteroids
7. Jupiter
8. Saturn
9. Uranus
10. Neptune
11. Pluto

Mercury

This is the eighth-largest planet in our Solar System, with a mass of 3.3 x 10^{23} kg and a diameter of 3,031 miles (4,878 km). It is the closest planet to the Sun, orbiting the latter at an average distance of only 36 million miles (58 million km; 0.38 that of the Earth's orbit).

Mercury's year is only 88 days long. Temperatures on the surface of the planet vary from −292°F to 800°F (−180 to 427 degrees C)—the widest variation in the entire Solar System.

Mercury's eccentric orbit means that if you were standing on its surface, you would see the Sun actually grow larger as it moved across

the sky. The Sun would then stop, reverse course briefly, halt once more, and then continue, shrinking all the while.

Incredibly, observations made by the Mariner 10 spacecraft on its missions in 1998 and 1999 suggest there may be frozen water in the shadowed areas at the poles, in spite of the searing heat.

Venus

The sixth-largest planet, Venus orbits the Sun at an average distance of 67 million miles (107.8 million km). It has a diameter of 7,515 miles (12,094 km) and a mass of 4.87×10^{24} kg. Its year is 225 days long—but its day is 243 days long!

Venus has a thick, opaque atmosphere that is 98 percent carbon dioxide, with clouds of sulphuric acid and sulphur. A runaway greenhouse effect makes it the hottest place in the Solar System, with temperatures of 878°F (470 degrees C), hot enough to melt lead, and pressures 90 times higher than on Earth. Although there was probably water on the surface at one time, it has long since boiled away.

Mars

Mars is 4,220 miles (6,791 km) in diameter and has a mass of 6.4×10^{23} kg. Its day is almost the same length as ours on Earth, but its year is 687 days long. The average surface temperature is a chilly −67°F (-55 degrees C), but Mars' elliptical orbit means that there are wide seasonal variations. Temperatures can drop to as low as −200°F (-129 degrees C) during winter, but reach a balmy 80°F (27 degrees C) during summer.

When it was much younger, Mars was probably very similar to Earth. However, most of its carbon dioxide was soaked up by rock, and, in the absence of plate tectonics, the carbon dioxide was never recycled. This prevented the generation of any significant greenhouse effect, leaving Mars cold, sterile, and inhospitable.

Although the atmosphere is thin, it can get very windy, with huge dust storms that can cover the entire planet for months on end.

Mars has two tiny moons, Phobos and Deimos.

Jupiter

Jupiter is more than twice as heavy as all of the other planets put together, and 318 times heavier than Earth. It is 88,820 miles (142,942 km) in diameter and has a mass of 1.9×10^{27} kg.

The planet is a huge ball of gas that gets denser the farther down you go, until you reach a rocky core about 10–15 times more massive than the Earth. Here, the temperature is 36,000°F (19,982 degrees C). Its atmosphere is 90 percent hydrogen and 10 percent helium, with traces of other substances, including methane, ammonia, and water. Surrounding the core, the pressure is so high—four million times higher than on the surface of the Earth—that hydrogen becomes a metallic liquid.

When you look at Jupiter, you are not seeing the surface at all, but the tops of enormous clouds that travel around the planet in alternating dark "belts" and light "zones," driven by winds of up to 400 mph (644 km/hr) traveling in opposing directions.

Jupiter has 61 known satellites, but new moons are being discovered all the time. The four largest—Io, Europa, Ganymede, and Callisto—were discovered by the Italian astronomer Galileo. Jupiter also has three faint rings.

Saturn

With a diameter of 74,860 miles (120,475 km) and a mass of 5.68×10^{26} kg, Saturn is the second-largest planet in our system. It is almost ten times farther away from the Sun than the Earth. It is most famous for its rings, which gave it a very odd appearance in the eyes of early astronomers, who couldn't figure out why it looked so peculiar. It was not until 1659 that Christiaan Huygens worked out what was going on.

Saturn is the least dense planet. Overall, its structure is like that of Jupiter, and it has similar light and dark bands in its atmosphere.

Saturn also has at least 31 moons, the largest being Titan.

Saturn's rings

Three rings are visible from Earth—A and B, separated by the Cassini Division, and C, which is much fainter—but the Voyager spacecraft, launched in 1977 and still traveling, discovered four more. The rings are made up of millions of particles of ice and some rocks, varying in size from just a fraction of an inch, to a few inches, to a mile (1.6 km). The rings are about 168,000 miles (270,370 km) in diameter but only a few miles thick.

Strange features of the rings include "spokes" (technically known as radial inhomogeneities), braids, and knots.

Uranus

With a diameter of 31,740 miles (51,081 km), Uranus is bigger than the next planet, Neptune, but has a smaller mass (of 8.68 x 10^{25} kg). It orbits the Sun once every 84 years. It is a ball of rock, ice, and gas (mainly hydrogen), shrouded in an atmosphere of yet more gas (83 percent hydrogen, 15 percent helium, and 2 percent methane, which absorbs red light, leavingUranus looking blue). It has 11 known rings and at least 21 moons, with names taken from William Shakespeare and Alexander Pope rather than classical mythology. The chief ones are Miranda, Ariel, Umbriel, Titania, and Oberon.

Neptune

Neptune is 30,745 miles (49,479 km) in diameter and 1.02 x 10^{26} kg in mass (17 times heavier than Earth). It was discovered in 1846 after two mathematicians predicted its orbit, but Galileo first noticed it in 1613—cloudy skies prevented him from identifying it definitively, and he assumed it was a star. It is similar in structure to Uranus, with high methane clouds that give it a blue color. It has at least three rings and 11 moons, of which Triton and Nereid are the best known.

Neptune has the strongest winds in the Solar System, blowing up to 1,250 mph (2,012 km). Its atmospheric features move pretty fast, too. One, nicknamed the Scooter, is a small white cloud that circulates the planet once every 16 hours.

Pluto

Pluto is so small that in 2006 it was reclassified as a dwarf planet. With a diameter of just 1,410 miles (2,269 km), it is smaller than our own Moon. Its orbit is highly eccentric, and sometimes it is nearer the Sun than Neptune. The surface temperature is around −364°F (-220 degrees C). Although composed mainly of rock and ice, there is speculation that the darker areas may be deposits of organic material.

Pluto's moon, Charon, is named in Greek myth after the ferryman who took souls to Hades (known as Pluto to the Romans), but may also be a nod to Sharon, wife of Jim Christy, who discovered it in 1971.

Most likely locations for life

Mars: fossils of bacteria may exist all over the planet. Current life might be found deep below the surface, where liquid water may exist. Certainly, bacteria exist in similar conditions on Earth.

Europa, one of Jupiter's moons: may have liquid water beneath its icy crust, while strong tides and magnetic activity could generate heat. The combination could produce conditions similar to those near Earth's mid-ocean vents.

Titan, Saturn's largest moon: has a smog-like atmosphere rich in organic chemicals similar to Earth's early atmosphere; it also has frozen water and a hot core.

Past Space Missions

All of the planets, with the sole exception of the dwarf planet Pluto—
at the farthest outpost of our Solar System—have now been visited by
humans in their quest to explore the great frontier of space. See the

Date	Name (nationality)	Mission objective	Mission outcome
October 4, 1957	*Sputnik 1* (USSR)	First Earth orbiter	Successfully completed
November 3, 1957	*Sputnik 2* (USSR)	First Earthling in space: Laika the dog!	Suffocated after a week in space
April 12, 1961	*Vostok 1* (USSR)	First man in space. Yuri Gagarin orbited Earth once	Successfully completed
June 16, 1963	*Vostok 6* (USSR)	First woman in space: Valentina Tereshkova	Successfully completed
March 18, 1965	*Voskhod 2* (USSR)	First spacewalk: Alexei Leonov	Successfully completed
July 16, 1969	*Apollo 11* (US)	First men on Moon: Neil Armstrong and Buzz Aldrin (also the men who have traveled farthest from Earth)	Successfully completed
November 14, 1969	*Apollo 12* (US)	Crewed lunar landing	Successfully completed
April 11, 1970	*Apollo 13* (US)	Attempted crewed lunar landing	Mechanical failure aborted mission—crew returned safely
August 17, 1970	*Venera 7* (USSR)	First Venus lander	Successfully completed
January 31, 1971	*Apollo 14* (US)	Crewed lunar landing	Successfully completed
July 26, 1971	*Apollo 15* (US)	Crewed lunar landing	Successfully completed
April 16, 1972	*Apollo 16* (US)	Crewed lunar landing	Successfully completed

chart below for details of all the major space trips carried out to date. A "Space Race" during the post–World War II years between the United States and the Soviet Union focused on putting man in orbit and ultimately on the Moon.

Date	Name (nationality)	Mission objective	Mission outcome
December 7, 1972	Apollo 17 (US)	Crewed lunar landing	Successfully completed
May 14, 1973	Skylab (US)	Space station (carried the first bathroom and first shower in space)	After successfully completing mission brief, burned up in atmosphere
August 20, 1975	Viking 1 (US)	Martian lander	Successfully completed
April 12, 1981	STS-1 Space Shuttle Columbia (US)	First shuttle mission: systems check	Successfully completed
July 2, 1985	Giotto (Europe)	Visited Halley's Comet	Successfully completed
January 28, 1986	STS-51-L Space Shuttle Challenger (US)	Deployment of tracking satellite and Halley's Comet observer	Exploded on launch, all astronauts lost
September 25, 1992	Mars Observer (US)	Mars orbiter	Contact lost
December 4, 1996	Mars Pathfinder (US)	Mars lander and rover	Successful
January 3, 1999	Mars Polar Lander (US)	Mars lander	Mission failure
January 16, 2003	STS-107 Space Shuttle Columbia (US)	16-day mission dedicated to research in physical, life, and space sciences	Exploded on re-entry, all astronauts lost

Current and Future Missions

Date	Name (nationality)	Mission objective	Status
August, 1977	Voyager 1 (US)	Jupiter and Saturn flyby	Successful and still in operation
September, 1977	Voyager 2 (US)	Jupiter, Saturn, Uranus, and Neptune flyby	Successful and still in operation
April 25, 1990	Hubble Telescope (US)	First and flagship mission of NASA's Great Observatories program	Initial flaw in mirror corrected by shuttle mission; Hubble still in operation
November 7, 1996	Mars Global Surveryor (US)	Mars orbiter	Still in operation
October 15, 1997	Cassini (US)	Saturn orbiter	Still in operation
October 15, 1997	Huygens (Europe) (onboard Cassini)	Titan Probe	Still in operation
July 3, 1998	Nozomi (Japan)	Orbital survey	Mission failure
April 7, 2001	Mars Odyssey (US)	Orbital survey	Still in operation
June 4, 2003	Mars Express (Europe)	Mars orbiter and lander (Beagle 2—UK)	Mission failure
June 10, 2003	Spirit (Mars Exploration Rover A) (US)	Mars Exploration Rover	Ceased communication in 2010
July 8, 2003	Opportunity (Mars Exploration Rover B) (US)	Mars Exploration Rover	Still in operation
September 28, 2003	Smart 1 (Europe)	Lunar probe	Deliberately crashed into Moon's surface in 2006
February 26, 2004	Rosetta (Europe)	Comet Rendezvous	Will reach comet by mid-2014
August 10-30, 2005	Mars Reconnaissance Orbiter (US)	Orbital survey	Attained Martian orbit in 2006

Date	Name (nationality)	Mission objective	Status
January 11, 2005	*Venus Express* (Europe)	Orbital survey	Arrived at Venus in 2006
October, 2007	*Kepler* (US) planet finder	Terrestrial	Launched in 2009
October-December, 2007	*Phoenix* (US) (water search)	Mars lander	Completed mission in 2008
October-December, 2009	*Mars Science Laboratory* (US)	Mars lander and rover	Landed on Mars in 2012
January 1, 2011	*BepiColombo* (Europe)	Mercury orbital survey	Completed orbital survey in 2012

Satellites

About 4,000 satellites have been launched into Earth's orbit, although many of them have since stopped working and/or fallen back into Earth's atmosphere and disintegrated.

First scientific satellite: *Sputnik 1, October 1957.*
First weather satellite: *Explorer 7, October 1959.*
First military (spy) satellite: *Discoverer 1, February 1959.*
First communications satellite: *ECHO-1, February 1962.*
First commercial telecommunications satellite: *TELSTAR, July 1962.*
First global positioning satellite: *November 1978.*

Messages to ET

Three main messages have been sent from Earth to any aliens who may be out there: the Pioneer messages; the Voyager messages; and the SETI message (sent by the Search for Extraterrestrial Intelligence Institute). Metal plaques affixed to Pioneers 10 and 11, which have now left the Solar System, identified their time and place of origin.

Voyagers 1 and 2 carried much more ambitious messages—gold-plated copper phonographs (records), which carry sounds and images to represent life on planet Earth. The records are encased in aluminium sleeves with instructions on how to play them and come complete with a cartridge and needle. The sleeves also carry the famous Voyager pictogram, showing naked humans and the location of our Solar System in relation to a number of pulsars.

Selected contents of the Voyager disc

Messages from the then US President Jimmy Carter and UN Secretary General Kurt Waldheim. **Recordings** of natural sounds (such as surf, thunder, and wind), animal sounds, and human-made sounds. **Greetings** in 55 different languages, from ancient Akkadian to the Chinese Wu dialect. **Musical tracks**, including: Bach's *Brandenburg Concerto*; pygmy girls' initiation song from the Congo; "Johnny B Goode" by Chuck Berry; Stravinsky's *Rite of Spring*; "Melancholy Blues" by Louis Armstrong and his Hot Seven; Azerbaijani bagpipe music; "Dark Was the Night" by Blind Willie Johnson. **Also**, 115 images, including scenes from daily life, watching TV, playing basketball.

The SETI Message

On November 16, 1974, the Arecibo radio telescope broadcast a radio message with codes for a complex diagram. This showed a human stick figure, the shape of the DNA molecule, the Solar System, and the radio telescope that sent the message.

On its wavelength, the SETI radio signal outshines the Sun and is a million times stronger than an ordinary TV signal. It was aimed at the M13 star cluster, 25,000 light years away, so it will take 25,000 years to get there. It will pass close to 30 other stars along the way.

Major UFO Sightings

Since the UFO craze began in 1947, over 100,000 people have reported seeing an unidentified flying object (usually interpreted as an alien spacecraft).

The Kenneth Arnold Sighting—June 1947. *Private pilot Kenneth Arnold reports seeing "a chain of nine peculiar-looking aircraft" that moved like "saucers skipping over water" above the Cascade Mountains of Washington state, in the northwest of the US. Anonymous headline writer coins the phrase "flying saucers."*

Roswell—July 1947. *Official military press release claims that a flying saucer has crashed in the Roswell region of New Mexico. The military subsequently blames a downed weather balloon. In the 1980s, the case is reopened by UFO researchers, who claim that witnesses have come forward to verify the original story.*

Valentich Incident—October 1978. *Australian pilot Frederich Valentich disappears over the Bass Strait between Tasmania and Australia, after reporting an encounter with a huge UFO. Aircraft never found.*

The Interrupted Journey—September 1961. *New Hampshire couple Barney and Betty Hill report a close encounter with a saucer-shaped UFO. Under hypnosis, they remember being abducted and probed. Although not the first reported abduction case, this was the first to receive widespread coverage.*

Travis Walton Case—November 1975. *Woodcutter Travis Walton is reported as having been abducted by UFO; he reappears a few days later with a lurid tale of a secret UFO base and probing.*

Rendlesham Forest—December 1980. *USAF base in Rendlesham Forest, Suffolk, UK, "buzzed" by strange lights. Airmen who investigate claim UFO sightings and encounters. Known as the British Roswell.*

The Brooklyn Bridge Abduction—November 1989. *Linda Cortile claims to have been beamed out of her New York apartment into a UFO, which plunges into the East River near the Brooklyn Bridge. Abduction supposedly verified by mysterious witnesses, who also claim to be bodyguards for the UN Secretary General, who is also abducted!*

The Close Encounters Scale

In 1972, J. Allen Hynek, a leading UFO expert, proposed a system of classification for UFO sightings and encounters, which included the famous "Close Encounter" (CE) scale. There are five CE categories (4 and 5 being more recent additions).

The scale, from low- to high-level contact, is as follows:

CE1: *Seeing objects or very brilliant lights from under 500 yards (457 m).*

CE2: *UFO physically affects the environment, leaving traces of its presence, such as sunburned witnesses or marks from landing gear.*

CE3: *Witnesses see or meet the occupants of the alien craft.*

CE4: *Witness goes into the spaceship (usually against his or her will).*

CE5: *Encounter involves paranormal elements, such as telepathy or poltergeist phenomena.*

Area 51

Area 51 is US government land in Nevada, north of Las Vegas. The area borders military installations such as the original atomic test site. It also contains a secret air force testing facility called Groom Lake Base. This was where top-secret airplanes, such as the U2 spy plane and the F-117A Stealth Fighter, were developed and test flown. Local aviators refer to the off-limits airspace around Area 51 as "Dreamland."

According to UFO buffs, Groom Lake Air Force Base is also home to the US government's secret UFO conspiracy. The chief claim is that scientists there are using crashed UFOs (for example, from Roswell) to "reverse engineer" advanced technologies.

What is the hard evidence for these claims? None.

THE
EARTH

Earth's Vital Statistics

Diameter at Equator: *7,923 miles (12,751 km).*

Diameter at the poles: *7,894 miles (12,704 km).*

Circumference at the Equator: *24,885 miles (40,049 km).*

Circumference at the poles: *24,796 miles (39,905 km).*

Mass: *5.94 x 10²⁴ kg.*

Age: *4.6 billion years.*

Distance from Sun: *92,919,254 miles (149.5 million km) or 8 light minutes.*

Time taken to orbit Sun: *365 days, 6 hours, 8 minutes.*

Time taken to rotate once on axis: *23 hours, 56 minutes.*

Total surface area: *196,936,000 sq miles (510 million sq km).*

Water area: *139,543,870 sq miles (361.4 million sq km) or 70.9 percent of surface area.*

Volume of water on Earth: *312,000,000 miles³ (1.3 billion cubic km).*

Land area: *57,392,606 sq miles (148.7 sq km) or 29.1 percent of surface area. If the Earth's surface were entirely level, it would be a smooth sphere completely covered by a continuous layer of seawater 8.812 feet (2.7 m) deep.*

Current human population: *7,103,442,000 (just over 7 billion).*

Speed of Earth's rotation at latitude of US/Europe/Japan: *~1,000 mph (1,609 km/hr).*

Speed of Earth's orbits round Sun: *66,700 mph (107,343 km/hr) or 18.5 miles (30 km)/second.*

Speed of Solar System's orbit around Galactic Central: *504,000 mph (811,110 km/hr) or 140 miles (225 km)/second.*

Life on Earth

Size and type of our Sun: *as a G2 spectral-class planet, our Sun provides enough heat and light but not too much radiation. It has also been around, and stable, for a very long time.*

Protective influence of Jupiter: *this planet acts as a massive shield, intercepting and deflecting asteroids and comets that would otherwise bombard the Earth so frequently that life could never have developed.*

Earth's magnetic field: *our planet generates a magnetic field that diverts the streams of potentially lethal ionized particles from the Sun into the Van Allen belts around the Earth.*

Earth's atmosphere: *plays a crucial role in allowing complex life to evolve. Firstly, it is thick enough to burn up the majority of asteroids before they can impact the surface. Secondly, it contains just the right amount of carbon dioxide to generate a mild Greenhouse Effect (GE).*

Earth's current average temperature, thanks to GE: *58°F (14.5 degrees C)*

Earth's average temperature without GE: *−6°F (-21 degrees C). Without this Greenhouse Effect, the oceans would freeze over.*

Liquid water: *the surface temperature of the Earth is in the correct range for water to exist as a liquid without boiling off into space. Liquid water is the only known medium in which life can flourish.*

Tectonic activity: *early in Earth's history, most of the carbon dioxide in the atmosphere combined with elements of the crust to form carbonate rocks. This prevented the GE from spiraling out of control and producing Venus-like conditions. On the other hand, if all the carbon dioxide had disappeared, there would be no GE and Earth would be cold and sterile, like Mars. Fortunately, plate tectonics provide a means of recycling carbon locked into rocks and putting just enough back into the atmosphere.*

Photosynthesis: *the evolution of photosynthesizing organisms led to the maintenance of high levels of oxygen in the atmosphere, allowing air-breathing creatures to evolve. The oxygen also generated an ozone layer, which helps to protect land organisms from damaging ultra-violet (UV) rays.*

Luck! Since life first evolved, the Earth has avoided any major cosmological disasters, such as getting sucked into a black hole, caught up in a supernova, or being hit by a small planet.

Composition of the Earth

The Earth is mainly iron (34.6 percent), most of which is locked in its core. Its crust contains silicon dioxide and other combinations of silicon (15.2 percent) and oxygen. Oxygen is the most abundant element in the crust, accounting for 29.5 percent of the Earth's total composition. The other elements that make up the Earth's composition are magnesium (12.7 percent), nickel (2.4 percent), sulphur (1.9 percent), and titanium (0.05 percent). The temperature at the core is 27,000,000°F (15 million degrees C)—hotter than the surface of the Sun.

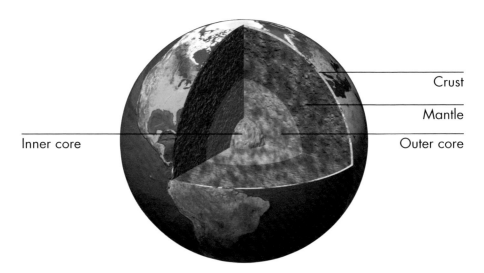

Inner core
Crust
Mantle
Outer core

Layers of the Earth

Layer	Average depth (miles)	Mass (in kg x 10²⁴)	Mass (percentage)
Crust	0–25 (0-40 km)	0.026 (+ atmosphere weighs 5 million trillion tons and oceans weigh 1,400 million trillion tons)	0.383
Mantle	25–1,750 (40-2,816 km)	4.043	69.6
Core	1,750–3,963 (2,816-6,378 km)	1.935	30

Geological Time Scale

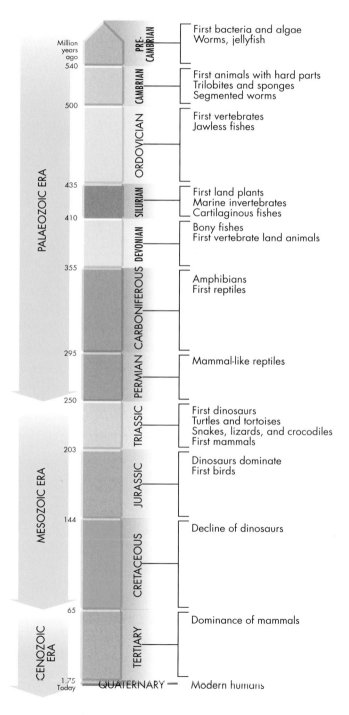

Million years ago	PRE-CAMBRIAN	First bacteria and algae Worms, jellyfish
540	CAMBRIAN	First animals with hard parts Trilobites and sponges Segmented worms
500	ORDOVICIAN	First vertebrates Jawless fishes
435	SILURIAN	First land plants Marine invertebrates Cartilaginous fishes
410	DEVONIAN	Bony fishes First vertebrate land animals
355	CARBONIFEROUS	Amphibians First reptiles
295	PERMIAN	Mammal-like reptiles
250	TRIASSIC	First dinosaurs Turtles and tortoises Snakes, lizards, and crocodiles First mammals
203	JURASSIC	Dinosaurs dominate First birds
144	CRETACEOUS	Decline of dinosaurs
65	TERTIARY	Dominance of mammals
1.75 Today	QUATERNARY	Modern humans

PALAEOZOIC ERA

MESOZOIC ERA

CENOZOIC ERA

The Poles

The Earth's magnetic field is generated by electric currents in its partially fluid mantle. Like a magnet, this field has poles. The geomagnetic pole is the point on the Earth's surface to which compass needles point, but its position is governed by the interaction of the magnetic field with the stream of charged particles given off by the Sun (via the Solar Wind) and the ionosphere in the upper atmosphere. This geomagnetic pole wanders and sometimes reverses.

Since early hominids evolved some 2.5 million years ago, there have been eight pole reversals. The most recent one was 690,000 years ago, but before then pole reversals were much more frequent—perhaps one is now overdue.

Latitude and Longitude

Lines of latitude and longitude are devices for arranging maps of the world into a grid system, whereby coordinates can be given for any point on the surface of the Earth. The lines are arranged with a scale

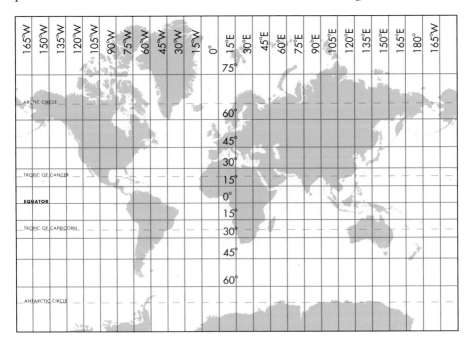

of degrees (°), which are subdivided into 60 minutes (noted as '), which are subdivided further into 60 seconds (noted as "). Latitude lines run horizontally, and longitude lines run vertically. A useful mnemonic is to visualize latitude lines as rungs in a ladder, and then remember the phrase "ladder-tude."

Latitude

Lines of latitude are called "parallels" because they run alongside one another. The Equator is said to be the line of 0° latitude, while the North Pole is 90° N and the South Pole is 90° S. Each degree is about 69 miles (111 km) apart.

Longitude

Because the Earth is a globe, the lines of longitude converge at the poles rather than running parallel to one another. At the Equator they are 69 miles (111 km) apart. They are also known as meridians.

When a map of the world is drawn in two dimensions, using the classic Mercator Projection, the longitude lines are drawn parallel to one another, which means that the areas between the lines at the top and bottom of the map have to be made to look broader than they actually are. This is why Greenland looks much bigger than it really is on most world maps, while the vast continent of Africa appears much smaller.

Using Coordinates

The coordinates for any point on the Earth's surface can be given as a combination of latitude and longitude. For example, Central Park, New York City, is located at 40° 47' N (of the Equator), 73° 58' W (of Greenwich). Even more precisely, the Capitol building in Washington, DC, is located at 38° 53' 23" N, 77° 00' 27" W.

OPPOSITE The world smoothed flat, with lines of latitude and longitude. In this projection, the US and Greenland appear disproportionately large.

Time Zones

The Prime Meridian, or 0° longitude, was set at Greenwich, UK (the location of the Royal Observatory), by an international conference in 1884. The lines of longitude go up to 180° E and W, where they meet at the International Date Line (IDL) on the opposite side of the

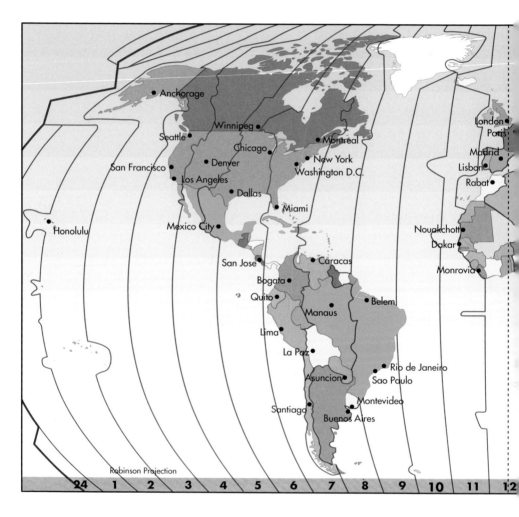

globe from Greenwich—although a look at the map reveals that the IDL has been given an irregular course to prevent giving different parts of Pacific island nations different dates.

Time zones west of Greenwich are "earlier" than Greenwich Mean Time (a.k.a. Coordinated Universal Time), and "later" east of it.

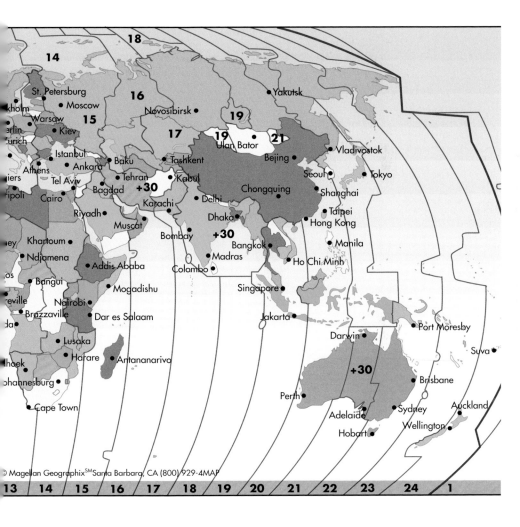

Atmospheric Zones

The Earth's atmosphere is 78.08 percent nitrogen, 20.95 percent oxygen, 0.93 percent argon, and 0.03 percent carbon dioxide.

Layer	Height (above Earth's surface)	Temperature	What do we know?
Troposphere	5 miles (8 km) at poles; 7 miles (11 km) at mid-latitudes; 10 miles (16 km) at Equator	Drops 3.6°F (2 degrees C) every 1,000 ft (305 m) up; minimum reaches −70°F (-57 degrees C)	Contains 75 percent of the total mass of the atmosphere. This is where life and almost all of our weather is found. The top of the troposphere is called the tropopause
Stratosphere	30 miles (48 km)	Stable at around −58°F (-50 degrees Celsius)	Contains 24 percent of the total mass of the atmosphere. At the bottom of the stratosphere is the ozone layer
Mesosphere	50 miles (80 km)	Decreases from 20°F at (-7 degrees C) base to −166°F, (-110 degrees C) before rising again at top	Meteors burn up in this zone to give "shooting stars;" together with the thermosphere, this layer contains many ionized particles, and they are collectively termed the ionosphere—this is the layer off which radio signals bounce to allow radio telecommunications
Thermosphere	400 miles (644 km)	Variable; can reach 1292°F (700 degrees C) but there are so few molecules, it would feel cold	Gets so hot because the thin atmosphere reabsorbs a lot of radiation that bounces back from the lower layers
Exosphere: together with thermosphere, makes up "outer atmosphere"	Up to 40,000 miles (64,374 km)	Falls to near zero (-18 degrees C)	The atmospheric density at 6,000 miles (9,656 km) is the same as outer space. Above this height, it is only the "atmosphere" in the sense that the Earth's gravitational and magnetic field exert some influence. The exosphere contains the magnetosphere, where the aurorae appear

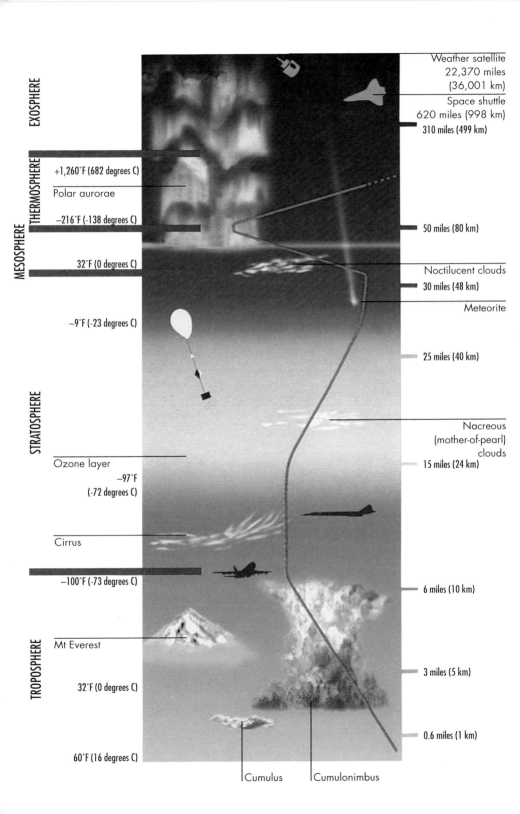

EXOSPHERE

THERMOSPHERE

MESOSPHERE

STRATOSPHERE

TROPOSPHERE

+1,260°F (682 degrees C)

Polar aurorae

−216°F (-138 degrees C)

32°F (0 degrees C)

−9°F (-23 degrees C)

Ozone layer

−97°F
(-72 degrees C)

Cirrus

−100°F (-73 degrees C)

Mt Everest

32°F (0 degrees C)

60°F (16 degrees C)

Weather satellite
22,370 miles
(36,001 km)
Space shuttle
620 miles (998 km)
310 miles (499 km)

50 miles (80 km)

Noctilucent clouds
30 miles (48 km)
Meteorite

25 miles (40 km)

Nacreous
(mother-of-pearl)
clouds
15 miles (24 km)

6 miles (10 km)

3 miles (5 km)

0.6 miles (1 km)

Cumulus

Cumulonimbus

Climate Zones

The most widely used climate classification scheme is the Köppen System, which designates climate types by letters, determined by each type's characteristic rainfall and temperatures.

There are six major climate types (designated by capital letters) and several subgroups (illustrated by lowercase letters added to the capital).

A **Moist Tropical Climates:** *high temperatures all year round; large amounts of rain all year.*

B **Dry Climates:** *little rain and a huge daily temperature range. Two subgroups: S (semiarid or steppe) and W (arid or desert).*

C **Humid Middle Latitude Climates:** *warm, dry summers, and cool, wet winters.*

D **Continental Climates:** *found in the interior regions of large landmasses. Total precipitation is low, and seasonal temperatures vary widely.*

E **Cold Climates:** *areas where permanent ice and tundra are always present, and only about four months of the year have temperatures above freezing.*

H **Highland Climates:** *specific to upland regions.*

Subgroups

f *Moist with adequate precipitation in all months, and no dry season. This letter usually accompanies the A, C, and D climates.*

m *Rainforest climate in spite of short, dry season in monsoon-type cycle. This letter only applies to A climates.*

s *Dry season in summer.*

w *Dry season in winter.*

(There are further subgroups, which show temperature variations.)

Earth's Biomes

A biome is a type of ecosystem. See the chart below for a summary of the 11 biomes that characterize the bulk of the world's landmass.

Biome	Climate Type	Köppen	Biome	Climate type	Köppen
Rainforest	Moist Tropical	Af	Deciduous forest	Moist Continental	Cf
Savanna	Wet-Dry Tropical	Aw	Taiga	Boreal Forest	Df
Desert	Dry Tropical	Bw	Tundra	Tundra	E
Steppe	Dry Mid-Latitude	Bs	Alpine	Highland	H
Chaparral	Mediterranean	Cs	Polar desert/ barrens	Polar-Arid/ Arctic-Alpine	E/EH
Grasslands	Dry Mid-Latitude	Bs			

Climate Extremes

Coldest: *Vostok, Antarctica—the temperature reached −138°F (-94 degrees C).*

Hottest: *Al Aziziyah, Libya—in 1922 it was 136°F (58 degrees C) in the shade.*

Fastest drop: *Brownrig, Montana, US—the temperature dropped from +44°F (7 degrees C) to −56°F (-49 degrees C) in one day.*

Fastest rise: *Spearfish, South Dakota, US—the temperature rose from −4°F (-20 degrees C) to +44°F (7 degrees C) in two minutes.*

Widest range: *Eastern Siberia—temperatures typically range from −76°F (-60 degrees C) to +99°F (37 degrees C).*

Climate Averages

Hottest place: *Dalol, Denakil Depression, Ethiopia—annual average temperature is 93.2°F (34 degrees C).*

Coldest place: *Plateau Station, Antarctica—annual average temperature is −134°F (-92 degrees C).*

Wettest place: *Mawsynram, Assam, India—annual average rainfall is 467.4 inches (1,187 cm).*

Driest place: *Atacama Desert, Chile—average annual rainfall is 0.03 inches (0.08 cm). This is the average over several years; in many years there is no recordable precipitation.*

Wind and Weather

The Beaufort Scale

The Beaufort Wind Scale was devised in 1805 by Sir Francis Beaufort, a rear admiral in the British navy, in order to describe the wind's effect on sailing ships. The scale (see chart below) is a series of numbers from 0 to 17, which indicate wind speed.

Number	Name	Wind speed (mph)	Number	Name	Wind speed (mph)
0	Calm	under 1 (1.6 km/hr)	7	Moderate gale	32–38 (51-61 km/hr)
1	Light air	1–3 (1.6-5 km/hr)	8	Fresh gale	39–46 (63-74 km/hr)
2	Light breeze	4–7 (6-11 km/hr)	9	Strong gale	47–54 (76-87 km/hr)
3	Gentle breeze	8–12 (13-19 km/hr)	10	Whole gale	55–63 (89-101 km/hr)
4	Moderate breeze	13–18 (21-29 km/hr)	11	Storm	64–73 (103-117 km/hr)
5	Fresh breeze	19–24 (31-39 km/hr)	12–17	Hurricane	74 (119 km/hr) and above
6	Strong breeze	25–31 (40-50 km/hr)			

Wind-chill Factor

Wind chill is a subjective measure of how cold it will feel given the absolute temperature and the wind speed. For example, a wind speed of 10 mph (16 km/hr) will make a temperature of 40°F (4 degrees C) feel more like an extremely chilly 28°F (–2 degrees C).

FACT! At around 435 miles (700 km) above the Earth's surface, the atmosphere becomes so thin that the average distance air molecules can travel without colliding is equal to the radius of the Earth.

The Ozone Hole

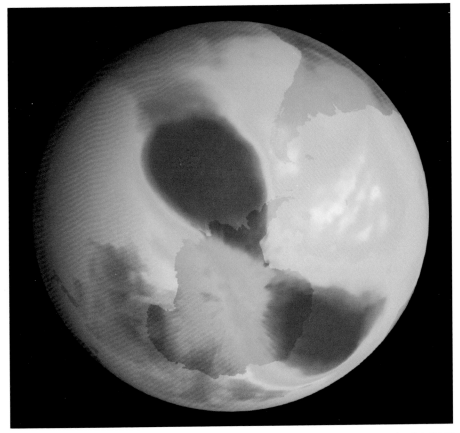

September 24, 2002

The so-called Ozone Hole is actually an area where the ozone layer is thinner and less dense than over the remainder of the globe. The Hole forms over the South Pole where air currents and low temperatures allow ozone-damaging chemicals (such as CFCs) to build up and eat away at the ozone.

Current research shows that while it has varied in size dramatically, currently it is at its biggest ever, covering the tip of South America and the Falklands, as well as parts of Antarctica. It reaches its greatest extent in October each year, then gradually shrinks in size over the following two months.

Plate Tectonics

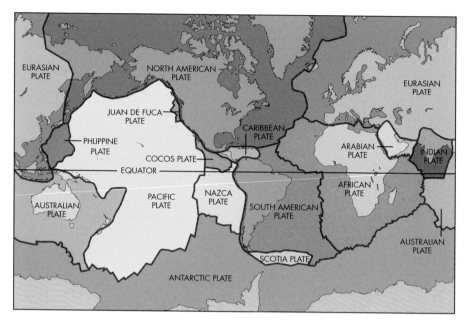

The surface of the Earth consists of a crust of solid rock floating on a bed of fluid magma (the mantle). This crust is separated into a number of interlocking plates.

The majority of the Earth's crust was formed through volcanic activity at plate boundaries. For instance, the mid-ocean ridge system—a network of volcanoes 25,000 miles (40,234 km) long—generates new oceanic crust at the rate of 4 miles³ (17 cubic km) per year, covering the ocean floor with basalt.

Here, with their locations, are the different types of plate boundary on Earth:

At constructive or spreading boundaries: *characterized by volcanic mid-ocean ridges or rift valleys, where magma wells up to create new plate material. Examples: the Great Rift Valley; the Mid-Atlantic Ridge.*

At destructive boundaries: *characterized by deep trenches, mountain ranges, and arcs of volcanoes and islands, where one plate "subducts" or dives under the other. Examples: the Aleutian Islands; the Andes.*

At **conservative boundaries:** *characterized by fault lines and heavy earthquake activity; the plates slide past one another, often in fits and starts. Example: the San Andreas Fault in California.*

At **compression boundaries:** *plates pile up to give mountain ranges. Example: the Himalayas.*

Volcanoes

At least 1,500 volcanoes are considered to be potentially active; 380 have erupted in this new century alone. In recent years, at least 15 have been in a state of virtually constant eruption.

About 50–60 volcanoes erupt every year. Every day, at least one volcano is erupting somewhere in the world.

Largest

The largest volcano in the world is Mauna Loa in Hawaii. If measured from its base on the seabed, it is the world's tallest mountain. It has a volume of about 9,600 miles^3 (40,015 cubic km), and an above-sea-level area of 1,978 sq miles (5,123 sq km).

Most Active

This is harder to establish, for it depends on how you define activity. In terms of major eruptions in recent times, Kilauea in Hawaii is said to be the most active volcano, having erupted more than 50 times since the late 18th century. In terms of length of continuous activity, Italy's Mts Etna and Stromboli have both been erupting nonstop for at least 2,500 years—and possibly for as long as 5,000 years.

FACT! Krakatau in Indonesia released tens of millions of tons of dust during its eruption in 1883. The resulting upper-air composition led to several years of global cooling and produced optical phenomena in the atmosphere. Mt Pinatubo in the Philippines erupted in 1991, spreading a belt of sulfur dioxide particles around the world, affecting the intensity of solar radiation.

Biggest Eruptions

One measure of the size of a volcanic eruption is the Volcanic Explosivity Index (VEI), a scale which goes up to eight. In historical times, the largest eruption was Tambora (Indonesia), in 1815, which had a VEI of seven—one of only four VEI7 eruptions in the last 10,000 years. At Tambora, about 9.6 miles³ (40 cubic km) of ash were blasted into the atmosphere, and 10,000 people were killed as a direct result of the eruption. Crop loss and famine claimed the lives of 80,000 more.

Combining VEI and destructivity in terms of loss of life, the five most dangerous eruptions in historical times are detailed below.

Location	Date	VEI	Casualties
Tambora, Indonesia	1815	7	92,000
Santorini, Greece	1628 BCE	6	Unknown (but probably destroyed the Minoan civilization)
Krakatoa, Indonesia	1883	6	36,400 (The eruption was heard 2,500 miles [4,023 km] away. A crater 4 miles [6 km] across was formed. Tsunami triggered by the eruption killed 36,000 people.)
Santa Maria, Guatemala	1902	6	6,000
Mt St Helens, US	1980	5	57

Biggest ever? It's hard to give accurate figures for prehistoric eruptions, but the consensus is that an eruption at Yellowstone 2,200,000 years ago was a VEI8 that ejected 600 miles³ (2,501 cubic km) of ash into the atmosphere (2,500 times more than Mt St Helens), making it the biggest ever.

Earthquakes

The Richter scale expresses the magnitude of an earthquake. Although not strictly a scale of effects or damage, the various Richter magnitudes are generally associated with different effects.

Richter magnitudes	Earthquake effects
Below 3.5	Generally not felt, but recorded
3.5–5.4	Often felt, but rarely causes damage
Below 6.0	At most, slight damage to well-designed buildings. Can cause major damage to poorly constructed buildings across small areas
6.1–6.9	Can be destructive in populated areas of up to about 62 miles (100 km) across
7.0–7.9	Major earthquake. Can cause serious damage over large areas
8 or greater	Great earthquake. Can cause serious damage in areas several hundred miles across

Major Earthquakes

The chart below shows the most destructive earthquakes ever recorded in terms of the number of deaths caused.

Date	Location	Fatalities	Magnitude
January 23, 1556	China, Shansi	830,000	~8
July 27, 1976	China, Tangshan	255,000 (official—possibly as many as 650,000)	7.5
August 9, 1138	Syria, Aleppo	230,000	Unknown
May 22, 1927	China, near Xining	200,000	7.9
December 22, 856	Iran, Damghan	200,000	Unknown

Mountains

If measured from the lowest point of its base, in the Hawaiian Trough on the floor of the Pacific Ocean, the dormant Hawaiian volcano Mauna Kea, at 13,796 ft (4,205 m) above sea level, is the tallest mountain in the world, with a total height of 33,476 ft (10,204 m).

Everest "grew" by 7 feet (2 m) in 1999; this was after GPS technology gave a more accurate measurement than had previously been possible.

Tallest Mountains on each Continent

Asia: *Mt Everest; 29,029 ft (8,848 m).*
South America: *Aconcagua; 22,834 ft (6,960 m).*
North America: *Mt McKinley; 20,320 ft (6,194 m).*
Africa: *Mt Kilimanjaro; 19,340 ft (5,895 m).*
Europe: *Mt Elbrus; 18,480 ft (5,633 m). Mt Elbrus is in the Caucasus range, near the border between Russia and Georgia; the highest mountain in Europe proper is Mont Blanc, in the Alps, at 15,771 ft (4,807 m).*
Oceania: *Puncak Jaya; 16,023 ft (4,884 m).*
Antarctica: *Vinson Massif; 16,863 ft (5,140 m).*
Australia: *Mt Kosciusko; 7,316 ft (2,230 m).*

Mountain Ranges

There are nine mountain ranges with peaks over 19,680 ft (5,998 m). They are, in descending order of highest peak: Himalayas; Karakoram; Kunlun; Andes; Tien-Shan; Gangdise; Hindu-Kush; Pamir; and Tanggula.

In descending height order, the longest ranges of mountains on Earth are as follows:

Andes, South America: *4,300 miles (6,920 km).*
Rocky Mountains, North America: *3,750 miles (6,035 km).*
Himalayas–Karakoram–Hindu Kush, Asia: *2,400 miles (3,862 km).*
Great Dividing Range, Australia: *2,250 miles (3,621 km).*
Trans-Antarctic Mountains, Antarctica: *2,200 miles (3,541 km).*

Impact Craters

Determining the size of impact craters on Earth is difficult and often controversial. Weathering and plate tectonics tend to obliterate most features over 300 million years old.

Largest Crater on Earth

Early in the life of the Solar System, there were many more large bodies hurtling around in near-Earth space than there are now, and one of these would have inflicted the largest-ever scar on the face of the Earth. (Curiously, one theory of the formation of the Moon suggests that it is made from material ejected from the Earth after a collision with another planet, and that the Pacific Basin is the hole left by the departing rock.)

In terms of craters that can still be detected, the 65-million-year-old Chicxulub crater, which lies beneath the Yucatan peninsula in Mexico, has an estimated diameter of 112–155 miles (180-249 km). It is the impact "scar" left by the asteroid, also known as the Cenote Ring, that is thought to have helped wipe out the dinosaurs. The asteroid was 12 miles (19 km) across (as broad as a mountain), and the impact had the force of 100 million megatons of TNT (equivalent to five billion atomic bombs).

Recently, scientists claim to have discovered an equally huge impact scar in South Africa—the two-billion-year-old Vredefort crater. According to some estimates, it could be as much as 211 miles (340 km) across.

Largest Crater off Earth

The Hellas Basin on Mars is about 930 miles (1,497 km) across. The recent impact of fragments of Comet Shoemaker-Levy 9 on Jupiter left a hole the size of Earth in the planet's gassy atmosphere.

Our Biosphere

Rainforests

The rainforests are incredible places, but few people can agree on the host of amazing facts and figures. Increasingly, conservation movements, scientists, and other experts dispute the data—no one doubts, though, that rainforests are among the most awe-inspiring places on Earth.

Biomass and Productivity

Only six percent of the Earth's land surface area is covered by rainforest, yet this type of habitat accounts for 80 percent of all land vegetation, and a third of all plant matter. A square yard (0.8 sq m) of rainforest can support between 99 and 176 lbs (45–80 kg) of living material or biomass and produce up to 8 lbs (4 kg) net biomass gain each year.

Biomass is the total mass of living matter found within a given area. So, for instance, the biomass of an acre of Amazonian rainforest tells you what the weight would be of all the wood, leaves, roots, seeds, vines, creepers, animals, moss, bacteria, etc., if it was collected and weighed as a single unit. Biomass can be used as a measure of the biological productivity of a type of habitat.

FACT! Rainforests support the greatest biodiversity of any ecosystem on the planet. According to conservationists, between 50 and 90 percent of all the Earth's species live in the rainforest, yet as many as 100 million species remain unidentified. Half an acre of rainforest may contain 200 species of tree, and over 40,000 species of insect, and over 600 new species of beetle have been discovered in studies of a single species of tree.

Rainforest Destruction
There is a huge debate about the actual rate of loss of rainforest, particularly where it applies to the Amazon, where it is claimed by some that logging and land clearance have slowed in recent decades.

According to conservationists, rainforest is being lost at the following rates:

- *An area the size of an American football field every second.*
- *75 acres every minute.*
- *100,000 acres a day.*
- *39 million acres every year—an area larger than the state of Michigan.*

Meanwhile, we are losing up to 270 species each day—the fastest rate of extinction since the last Ice Age (although, once again, this figure is contentious).

Desertification and Soil Loss
The loss of soil and the degradation of arable land into semidesert are huge and spiraling global problems, particularly since the soil removed by wind or water is 1.3 to 5 times richer in organic matter than the soil left behind.

Area of worst soil loss on planet: *China; middle reaches of Yellow River/upper reaches of Yangtze River.*
Annual topsoil load of Yellow River: *1.6 billion tons.*
Area of arable land destroyed and abandoned annually because of unsustainable farming practices: *Between 15 and 30 million acres.*
Area of arable land already lost to erosion: *2.47 billion acres, equivalent to one-twelfth of the Earth's entire land surface. Over the last 20 years, an area equivalent to all of the arable land in America has been lost.*

Soil erosion rates are highest in Asia, Africa, and South America, where an average of 30–40 tonnes of soil are lost per acre per year—twice as much as in the US and Europe.

Oceans

There used to be only four oceans, but in 2000 the International Hydrographic Organization approved the Southern Ocean as the fourth largest, pushing the Arctic Ocean to the bottom of the list.

By Size

Name	Size (sq miles)	Bordering continents
Pacific	60,060,000 (155.6 million sq km)	America, Australia, Asia
Atlantic	29,637,800 (76.8 million sq km)	America, Africa, Europe
Indian	26,469,470 (68.6 million sq km)	Africa, Asia
Southern	7,848,250 (20.3 million sq km)	Oceania, America, Africa, Australia
Arctic	5,427,020 (14.1 million sq km)	America, Asia

Even though the Arctic is the smallest ocean, with just one percent of the Earth's seawater, it still holds 25 times more water than all of the fresh water in the world.

Greatest Depths

The deepest place on the Earth's surface is the Mariana Trench, which is situated in the Pacific. It is 35,827 ft (10,920 m) deep—1.24 miles (2 km) deeper than Mt Everest is tall. According to some estimates, the deepest point of the Mariana Trench, known as the Challenger Deep, is 36,188 ft (11,030 m) below sea level.

The Atlantic Ocean reaches a depth of 30,246 ft (9,219 m) in the Puerto Rico Trench. The deepest point in the Caribbean is 22,788 ft (6,946 m), while the Mediterranean reaches a depth of 15,197 ft (4,632 m) off Southern Greece.

Salinity of the Oceans

Salts of many different elements are dissolved in the world's oceans and seas. The solid mass of all these salts could be as great as 50,000,000,000,000,000 tonnes.

If it were extracted from the water and spread over the Earth's land surface, it would form a continuous layer over 500 ft (152 m) thick—the height of a 40-story office block.

The Fate of the Oceans

As the Sun grows older, it will gradually increase in brightness, and the Earth will heat up. In approximately 500 million years, the oceans will heat up to 140°F (60 degrees C) and atmospheric moisture content will rocket. This water will migrate into the stratosphere and, from there, into the upper atmosphere and into space. By about one billion years from now, the oceans will have entirely boiled away.

Biggest wave The highest-ever-recorded tsunami (a tidal wave created by an earthquake) was 210 ft (64 m) above sea level (about 18 storeys high). It hit the Kamchatka Peninsula, on the eastern coast of Siberia, in 1737.

Phytoplankton

It is estimated that human activities pump 7 billion tonnes of carbon into the atmosphere. But, as a counterbalancing effect, 3–4 billion tonnes of this are fixed by oceanic phytoplankton (photosynthesizing plant plankton). Annually, 550 million tonnes of phytoplankton grow in the Southern Ocean alone.

According to some scientific estimates, oceanic plant life generates 30–40 percent of the oxygen that replenishes the stocks in the Earth's atmosphere.

Ice and the Oceans

There is as much ice in Antarctica (7.2 million cubic miles; 30 million cubic km) as there is water in the Atlantic Ocean.

If all the ice at the Earth's poles were to melt, the world sea level would rise between 500 and 600 ft (152–183 m). As a result, 85 to 90 percent of the Earth's surface would be covered with water (the current figure is 70.9 percent). In the US, a new sea would be created that would stretch along the course of the Mississippi, from the Great Lakes to the Gulf of Mexico.

Icebergs

The Arctic produces 10,000 to 50,000 icebergs every year. Icebergs usually take four years to melt.

The largest-ever iceberg was sighted in the waters of the South Pacific in 1956. It was 208 miles (335 km) long and 60 miles (97 km) wide—roughly the size of Belgium.

Pollution and the Oceans

Each year, the amount of trash dumped into the world's oceans is three times higher than the mass of fish taken out of them.

A single quart of motor oil can contaminate up to 2 million gallons (7.6 million l) of drinking water. When the *Exxon Valdez* ran aground off Alaska, 42,000 tons of oil were spilt (equivalent to 125 Olympic-sized swimming pools). The worst-ever oil-tanker disaster was on July 19, 1979, when the *Atlantic Empress* collided with the *Aegean Captain* off the coast of Tobago, releasing 275,577 tons of oil into the sea.

Between 1994 and 1998, the most recent years for which records could be obtained, marine salvage workers recovered 6,847,000 tonnes of oil, 421,954 tonnes of hazardous chemicals, and 202,870 tonnes of other pollutants from the oceans.

Rivers, Lakes, and Waterfalls

River	Continent	Length (miles)
Nile	Africa	4,239 (6,822 km)
Amazon	South America	3,998 (6,434 km)
Chang Jiang (a.k.a. Yangtze-Kiang)	Asia	3,963 (6,378 km)
Mississippi (incl. Missouri and Red Rock)	North America	3,709 (5,969 km)
Yenisey-Angara	Asia	3,439 (5,535 km)

The World's Biggest Lakes

Sea	Continent	Length (sq miles)
Caspian Sea	Asia–Europe	143,000 (370,368 sq km)
Superior	North America	31,700 (82,102 sq km)
Victoria	Africa	26,828 (69,484 sq km)
Huron	North America	23,010 (59,596 sq km)
Michigan	North America	22,320 (57,809 sq km)
Tanganyika	Africa	12,700 (32,893 sq km)
Baikal	Asia	12,160 (31,494 sq km)
Great Bear	North America	12,096 (31,328 sq km)
Malawi	Africa	11,160 (28,904 sq km)
Aral Sea	Asia	11,000 (28,490 sq km)

The World's Longest Rivers

Lake Baikal, in Russia, is the deepest lake in the world, reaching 5,315 ft (1,620 m). It contains one-fifth of the world's liquid freshwater reserves. It would take all the rivers of the world nearly one year to fill Lake Baikal's basin.

The World's Highest Waterfalls

Falls	Place	Height (ft)
Angel	Canaima National Park, Venezuela	3,212 (979 m)
Tugela	Natal NP, South Africa	2,800 (853 m)
Utigord	Nesdale, Norway	2,625 (800 m)
Mongefossen	Marstein, Norway	2,540 (774 m)
Mutarazi	Nyanga NP, Zimbabwe	2,499 (762 m)
Yosemite	Yosemite NP, US	2,425 (739 m)

Doomsday Scenarios

The number of ways in which modern civilization could be brought crashing down seems to increase by the day. Here are the top 10 doomsday scenarios, each followed by a risk-assessment rating.

Ecological Meltdown

Many parts of the world face an imminent water crisis, with dwindling resources constantly being stretched farther and farther. Water wars may well break out in the future. This water crisis is exacerbating the terrible problems of soil loss and desertification, which are worsened by the increasing salination of many soils around the world.

However, all this could just be the tip of the iceberg—as the developing world tries to increase consumption and quality of life to developed-world levels, the Earth faces drastically worsening problems of pollution, habitat destruction, overfishing, population pressure, and so forth. Research shows that the global ecosystem can probably absorb a lot of damage without changing drastically, but above a certain threshold, it will inevitably—and suddenly—collapse. Results? Drought, famine, disease, disaster.

Risk assessment: *7/10*

Third World War

Worsening worldwide poverty and injustice, and an increasing gap between the haves and have-nots, may lead to mass migration and will increase global instability. With weapons of mass destruction scattered around the world, an apocalyptic showdown could happen.

Risk assessment: *6/10*

Climate Change

The phenomenon of global warming is now generally accepted. A less well-known risk is the advent of another Ice Age, either globally (one is overdue) or locally, around the Atlantic, because of the imminent failure of the polar ocean "shunt" that drives the Gulf

Stream. Increasing climate instability makes both outcomes more likely and will probably lead to worsening weather disasters, boosting the likelihood of scenarios 1 and 2.

Risk assessment: *5/10*

The Frankenstein Effect

As scientific and technological advances outstrip social controls, the chances of humankind being undone by its own inventions increase. Risk areas include: nanotechnology (where micromachines could replicate uncontrollably); global super-plagues (caused by a combination of antibiotic-resistant bugs, genes leaking from genetically modified species, and biological warfare); creeping pollution of the food chain by toxic material; Y2K-style computer bugs bringing down the world's IT systems; electromagnetic pollution from mobile phones and other sources, which could cause widespread cancers; and the spiraling impact of diseases of "civilization" such as obesity and diabetes.

There is even a risk of physicists setting off chain reactions they can't control, as scientists continue to investigate the fundamental forces of the universe.

Risk assessment: *2/10*

Giant Asteroid/Comet Strike

This is the most obvious and popular doomsday scenario, but may not actually be that likely. Given sufficient warning, the world should, in theory, have the resources to protect itself, particularly as technology improves.

Risk assessment: *1/10*

Massive Volcanic Eruption

A truly stupendous volcanic eruption could cause a "nuclear winter" effect, complete with acid rain and poisoned oceans.

Risk assessment: *below 1/10*

Mega-Tsunami

A huge landslide into the ocean could create a ring of massive waves that would obliterate every city on the surrounding seaboards. The prime candidate is one of the Canary Islands, where a huge volcanic rift threatens to topple half of the island into the sea and drown the East Coast of the US, and possibly, the western coast of Europe, with global consequences.

Risk assessment: *below 1/10*

Thinning Ozone

Scientists are divided over whether the ban on CFCs has worked. The year 2006 saw the biggest-ever ozone hole (actually a region where the ozone layer is thinner than usual), while the ozone layer around the rest of the world may also be thinning, increasing humankind's exposure to ultra-violet (UV) rays and causing rocketing rates of skin cancer. If it gets much worse, surface life may not be sustainable.

Risk assessment: *below 1/10*

Cosmological Catastrophe

A wandering black hole, a nearby supernova, or a cosmic shock wave produced by some as-yet-unknown mechanism would spell certain doom for life on Earth, but seems unlikely.

Risk assessment: *below 1/10*

Pole Reversal

A favorite of doomsday prophets. But even if a pole reversal were likely, which is far from certain, it probably wouldn't have a catastrophic effect on civilization.

Risk assessment: *below 1/10*

NATIONS
OF THE WORLD

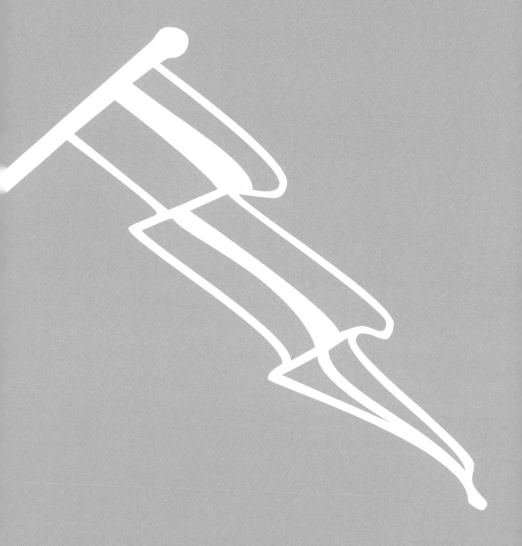

Countries

The world's nations are listed below with data on their size, population, and Gross Domestic Product rate. Each nation's capital and main language are also given. Only recognized nation-states are included—dependent territories are not listed, with a very few significant exceptions (such as Bermuda and the Faeroe Isles).

Nation	Area (sq miles)	Population	GDP*	Capital	Main languages
Afghanistan	250,001	26,813,057	$21,000	Kabul	Pushtu and Dari
Albania	11,100	3,510,484	$10,500	Tirana	Albanian
Algeria	919,594	31,736,053	$171,000	Algiers	Arabic and Berber
Andorra	181	67,627	$1,200	Andorra la Vella	Catalan
Angola	481,353	10,366,031	$10,100	Luanda	Portuguese and Bantu-languages
Antigua and Barbuda	171	66,970	$533	St. John's	English
Argentina	1,068,301	37,384,816	$476,000	Buenos Aires	Spanish
Armenia	11,506	3,336,100	$10,000	Yerevan	Armenian
Australia	2,967,907	19,357,594	$445,800	Canberra	English
Austria	32,378	8,150,835	$203,000	Vienna	German
Azerbaijan	33,436	7,771,092	$23,500	Baku	Azeri
Bahamas, The	5,382	297,852	$4,500	Nassau	English
Bahrain	239	645,361	$10,100	Al-Manámah	Arabic
Bangladesh	55,599	131,269,860	$203,000	Dhaka	Bengali
Barbados	166	275,330	$4,000	Bridgetown	English
Belarus	80,155	10,350,194	$78,800	Minsk	Belarussian and Russian
Belgium	11,780	10,258,762	$259,200	Brussels	Flemish and French

★ *Gross Domestic Product*

Nation	Area (sq miles)	Population	GDP*	Capital	Main languages
Belize	8,867	256,062	$790	Belmopan	English
Benin	43,483	6,590,782	$6,600	Porto-Novo	French and African languages
Bermuda	23	63,503	$2,100	Hamilton	English
Bhutan	18,147	2,049,412	$2,300	Thimphu	Dzongkha
Bolivia	424,164	8,300,463	$20,900	La Paz	Spanish, Quechua, and Aymara
Bosnia and Herzegovina	19,741	3,922,205	$6,500	Sarajevo	Serbian, Bosnian, Croatian
Botswana	231,804	1,586,119	$10,400	Gaborone	Setswana and English
Brazil	3,286,486	174,468,575	$1,130,000	Brasília	Portuguese
Brunei	2,228	343,653	$5,900	Bandar Seri Begawan	Malay
Bulgaria	42,823	7,707,495	$48,000	Sofia	Bulgarian
Burkina Faso	105,869	12,272,289	$12,000	Ouagadougou	French and African languages
Burundi	10,745	6,223,897	$4,400	Bujumbura	Kirundi, Swahili, and French
Cambodia	69,900	12,491,501	$16,100	Phnom Penh	Khmer
Cameroon	183,568	15,803,220	$26,000	Yaoundé	French and English
Canada	3,851,806	31,592,805	$774,700	Ottawa, Ontario	English and French
Cape Verde	1,557	405,163	$670	Praia	Portuguese and Crioulo
Central African Republic	240,535	3,576,884	$6,100	Bangui	Sangho and French
Chad	495,755	8,707,078	$8,100	N'Djamena	French and Arabic
Chile	292,260	15,328,467	$153,100	Santiago	Spanish
China	3,705,404	1,273,111,290	$4,500,000	Beijing	Chinese
Colombia	439,735	40,349,388	$250,000	Bogotá	Spanish

continued…

Nation	Area (sq miles)	Population	GDP*	Capital	Main languages
Comoros	838	596,202	$419	Moroni	Comoran, Arabic, and French
Congo, Democratic Republic of the	905,567	53,624,718	$31,000	Kinshasa	French and Lingala
Congo-Brazzaville Republic of the	132,047	2,894,336	$3,100	Brazzaville	French, Chiluba, Kikongo, Lingala, and Swahili
Cook Islands	93	20,611	$100	Avarua	English and Cook Islands Maori
Costa Rica	19,730	3,773,057	$25,000	San José	Spanish
Côte d'Ivoire	124,502	16,393,221	$26,200	Yamoussoukro (official)	French
Croatia	21,831	4,334,142	$24,900	Zagreb	Croatian
Cuba	42,803	11,184,023	$19,200	Havana	Spanish
Cyprus	3,571	762,887	$10,530	Nicosia	Greek and Turkish (in North Cyprus)
Czech Republic	30,450	10,264,212	$132,400	Prague	Czech
Denmark	16,639	5,352,815	$136,200	Copenhagen	Danish
Djibouti	8,494	460,700	$574	Djibouti	Arabic and French
Dominican Republic	18,815	8,581,477	$48,300	Santo Domingo	Spanish
East Timor	5,743	952,618	N/A	Dili	Tetum
Ecuador	109,483	13,183,978	$37,200	Quito	Spanish and Quechua
Egypt	386,662	69,536,644	$247,000	Cairo	Arabic
El Salvador	8,124	6,237,662	$24,000	San Salvador	Spanish
Equatorial Guinea	10,831	486,060	$960	Malabo	Fang, Bubi, Spanish, and French
Eritrea	46,842	4,298,269	$2,900	Asmara	Tigrinya and Arabic
Estonia	17,462	1,423,316	$14,700	Tallinn	Estonian and Russian
Ethiopia, Federal Democratic Republic of	435,186	65,891,874	$39,200	Addis Ababa	Amharic and Tigrinya

* Gross Domestic Product

Nation	Area (sq miles)	Population	GDP*	Capital	Main languages
Faeroe Islands	540	45,661	$910	Torshavn	Faeroic and Danish
Fiji	7,054	844,330	$5,900	Suva (on Viti Levu)	Fijian, Hindi, and English
Finland	130,128	5,175,783	$118,300	Helsinki	Finnish and Swedish
France	211,209	59,551,227	$1,448,000	Paris	French
French Guiana	35,135	177,562	$1,000	Cayenne	French
Gabon	103,347	1,221,175	$7,700	Libreville	French, Fang, and Bantu languages
Gambia, The	4,363	1,411,205	$1,500	Banjul	English and Mandinka
Georgia	26,911	4,989,285	$22,800	Tbilisi	Georgian
Germany	137,846	83,029,536	$1,936,000	Berlin (capital since Oct 1999)	German
Ghana	92,101	19,894,014	$37,400	Accra	English, Ewe, and Ga
Greece	50,942	10,623,835	$181,900	Athens	Greek
Grenada	131	89,227	$394	St. George's	English
Guatemala	42,043	12,974,361	$46,200	Guatemala City	Spanish
Guinea	94,926	7,613,870	$10,000	Conakry	French
Guinea-Bissau	13,946	1,315,822	$1,100	Bissau	Portuguese and Crioulo
Guyana	83,000	697,181	$3,400	Georgetown	English and Hindi
Haiti	10,714	6,964,549	$12,700	Port-au-Prince	French and Creole
Honduras	43,278	6,406,052	$17,000	Tegucigalpa	Spanish
Hungary	35,919	10,106,017	$113,900	Budapest	Hungarian
Iceland	39,768	277,906	$6,850	Reykjavik	Icelandic
India	1,269,345	1,029,991,145	$2,200,000	Delhi	Hindi, English, and 17 regional languages
Indonesia	741,099	228,437,870	$654,000	Jakarta	Bahasa Indonesia and Javanese

continued…

Nation	Area (sq miles)	Population	GDP*	Capital	Main languages
Iran	636,296	66,128,965	$413,000	Tehran	Farsi, Turkic, and Kurdish
Iraq	168,754	23,331,985	$57,000	Baghdad	Arabic
Ireland	27,135	3,840,838	$81,900	Dublin	English and Irish
Israel	8,019	5,938,093	$110,200	Jerusalem	Hebrew and Arabic
Italy	116,305	57,679,825	$1,273,000	Rome	Italian
Jamaica	4,243	2,665,636	$9,700	Kingston	English
Japan	145,883	126,771,662	$3,150,000	Tokyo	Japanese
Jordan	35,637	5,153,378	$17,300	Amman	Arabic
Kazakhstan	1,049,155	16,731,303	$85,600	Astana	Russian and Kazakh
Kenya	224,962	30,765,916	$45,600	Nairobi	Swahili, English, Kikuyo, and Luo
Kiribati	277	94,149	$76	Tarawa	i-Kiribati and English
Korea, North	46,541	21,968,228	$22,000	Pyongyang	Korean
Korea, South	38,023	47,904,370	$764,600	Seoul	Korean
Kuwait	6,880	2,041,961	$29,300	Kuwait	Arabic
Kyrgyzstan	76,641	4,753,003	$12,600	Bishkek (formerly Frunze)	Kyrgyz and Russian
Laos	91,429	5,635,967	$9,000	Vientiane	Lao
Latvia	24,938	2,385,231	$17,300	Riga	Latvian and Russian
Lebanon	4,015	3,627,774	$18,200	Beirut	Arabic
Lesotho	11,720	2,177,062	$5,100	Maseru	Sesotho and English
Liberia	43,000	3,225,837	$3,350	Monrovia	English
Libya	679,362	5,240,599	$45,400	Tripoli	Arabic
Liechtenstein	62	32,528	$730	Vaduz	German
Lithuania	25,174	3,610,535	$26,400	Vilnius	Lithuanian, Russian, and Polish
Luxembourg	998	442,972	$15,900	Luxembourg	Luxembourgish

★ *Gross Domestic Product*

Nation	Area (sq miles)	Population	GDP*	Capital	Main languages
Macedonia, The Former Yugoslav Republic of	9,781	2,046,209	$9,000	Skopje	Macedonian and Albanian
Madagascar	226,657	15,982,563	$12,300	Antananarivo	Malagasy and French
Malawi	45,745	10,548,250	$9,400	Lilongwe	Chichewa and English
Malaysia	127,317	22,229,040	$223,700	Kuala Lumpur	Malay and Chinese
Maldives	116	310,764	$594	Malé	Dhivehi
Mali	478,766	11,008,518	$9,100	Bamako	Bambara and French
Malta	122	394,583	$5,600	Valletta	Maltese and English
Marshall Islands	70	70,822	$105	Majuro	English and Marshallese
Mauritania	397,955	2,747,312	$5,400	Nouakchott	Arabic and French
Mauritius	718	1,189,825	$12,300	Port Louis	Mauritian (Creole), Bhojipuri, English, and French
Mexico	761,605	101,879,171	$915,000	Mexico City	Spanish
Micronesia, Federated States of	271	134,597	$263	Palikir	English
Moldova	13,067	4,431,570	$11,300	Chisinau	Russian and Moldovan
Monaco	1	31,842	$870	Monaco	French
Mongolia	604,249	2,654,999	$4,700	Ulaan Baatar	Mongolian
Morocco	172,414	30,645,305	$105,000	Rabat	Arabic and Berber
Mozambique	309,495	19,371,057	$19,100	Maputo	Portuguese and Swahili
Myanmar	261,970	41,994,678	$63,700	Rangoon	Burmese
Namibia	318,695	1,797,677	$7,600	Windhoek	English, Bantu languages, Afrikaans, and German
Nauru	8	12,088	$59	Yaren	English and Nauruan

continued…

Nation	Area (sq miles)	Population	GDP*	Capital	Main languages
Nepal	54,363	25,284,463	$33,700	Kathmandu	Nepali
Netherlands	16,033	15,981,472	$388,400	Amsterdam (official), The Hague (administrative capital)	Dutch
New Zealand	103,738	3,864,129	$67,600	Wellington	English and Maori
Nicaragua	49,998	4,918,393	$13,100	Managua	Spanish
Niger	489,191	10,355,156	$10,000	Niamey	Hausa, Djerma, and French
Nigeria	356,669	126,635,626	$117,000	Abuja	English, Yoruba, Igbo, and Hausa
Norway	125,182	4,503,440	$124,100	Oslo	Norwegian
Oman	82,031	2,622,198	$19,600	Muscat	Arabic
Pakistan	310,403	144,616,639	$282,000	Islamabad	Punjabi, Urdu, Pushtu, and Sindhi
Palau	177	19,092	$129	Koror	Palau and English
Palestine (proposed state)	N/A	N/A	N/A	East Jerusalem	Arabic
Panama	30,193	2,845,647	$16,600	Panama City	Spanish
Papua New Guinea	178,703	5,049,055	$12,200	Port Moresby	English and Pidgin English
Paraguay	157,047	5,734,139	$26,200	Asunción	Spanish
Peru	496,226	27,483,864	$123,000	Lima	Spanish, Quechua
Philippines	115,831	82,841,518	$310,000	Manila	Filipino, Tagalog, and Cebuano
Poland	120,728	38,633,912	$327,500	Warsaw	Polish
Portugal	35,672	10,066,253	$159,000	Lisbon	Portuguese
Qatar	4,416	769,152	$15,100	Doha	Arabic
Romania	91,699	22,364,022	$132,500	Bucharest	Romanian
Russia	6,592,767	145,470,197	$1,120,000	Moscow	Russian

* *Gross Domestic Product*

Nation	Area (sq miles)	Population	GDP*	Capital	Main languages
Rwanda	10,169	7,312,756	$6,400	Kigali	Kinyarwanda, French, and English
Saint Kitts and Nevis	101	38,756	$274	Basseterre (on St. Kitts)	English and Creole-English
Saint Lucia	239	158,178	$700	Castries	English and Patois
Saint Vincent and the Grenadines	150	115,942	$322	Kingstown	English and Creole-English
Samoa	1,104	179,058	$571	Apia	Samoan and English
San Marino	24	27,336	$860	San Marino	Italian
São Tomé and Principe	386	165,034	$178	São Tomé	Portuguese and Crioulo
Saudi Arabia	756,984	22,757,092	$232,000	Riyadh	Arabic
Senegal	75,749	10,284,929	$16,000	Dakar	Wolof, French, and Mande languages
Serbia and Montenegro	39,518	10,677,290	$24,200	Belgrade	Serbian
Seychelles	176	79,715	$610	Victoria	Creole and English
Sierra Leone	27,699	5,426,618	$2,700	Freetown	English, Mende, Temne, and Krio
Singapore	250	4,300,419	$109,800	Singapore	Chinese, Malay, and English
Slovakia	18,859	5,414,937	$55,300	Bratislava	Slovak and Hungarian
Slovenia	7,820	1,930,132	$22,900	Ljubljana	Slovenian
Solomon Islands	10,985	480,442	$900	Honiara (on Guadalcanal)	English and Pidgin English
Somalia	246,201	7,488,773	$4,300	Mogadishu	Somali
South Africa	471,010	43,586,097	$369,000	Pretoria	English, Afrikaans, Zulu, Xhosa, and other African languages
Spain	194,897	40,037,995	$720,800	Madrid	Spanish, Catalan, and Basque

continued...

Nation	Area (sq miles)	Population	GDP*	Capital	Main languages
Sri Lanka	25,332	19,408,635	$62,700	Colombo	Sinhala and Tamil
Sudan	967,498	36,080,373	$35,700	Khartoum	Arabic and African languages
Suriname	63,039	433,998	$1,480	Paramaribo	Dutch and Sranan Tongo
Swaziland	6,704	1,104,343	$4,400	Mbabane	Siswati and English
Sweden	173,732	8,875,053	$197,000	Stockholm	Swedish
Switzerland	15,942	7,283,274	$207,000	Bern	German, French, and Italian
Syria	71,498	16,728,808	$50,900	Damascus	Arabic
Taiwan	13,892	22,370,461	$386,000	Taipei	Chinese
Tajikistan	55,251	6,578,681	$7,300	Dushanbe	Tajik and Russian
Tanzania	364,900	36,232,074	$25,100	Dar es Salaam, (Official capital) Dodoma	Kiswahili and English
Thailand	198,456	61,797,751	$413,000	Bangkok	Thai
Togo	21,925	5,153,088	$7,300	Lomé	French, Ewe, and Kabyé
Tonga	289	104,227	$225	Nuku'alofa	Tongan and English
Trinidad and Tobago	1,980	1,169,682	$11,200	Port-of-Spain	English
Tunisia	63,170	9,705,102	$62,800	Tunis	Arabic and Berber
Turkey	301,383	66,493,970	$444,000	Ankara	Turkish and Kurdish
Turkmenistan	188,456	4,603,244	$19,600	Ashgabat	Turkmen
Tuvalu	10	10,991	$12	Fongafale	Tuvaluan and English
Uganda	91,135	23,985,712	$26,200	Kampala	English, Banyor, and other African languages
Ukraine	233,090	48,760,474	$189,400	Kyiv (Kiev)	Ukrainian and Russian
United Arab Emirates	32,000	2,407,460	$54,000	Abu Dhabi	Arabic

* Gross Domestic Product

Nation	Area (sq miles)	Population	GDP*	Capital	Main languages
United Kingdom	94,525	59,647,790	$1,360,000	London	English
United States of America	3,717,810	278,058,881	$9,963,000	Washington, DC	English and Spanish
Uruguay	68,039	3,360,105	$31,000	Montevideo	Spanish
Uzbekistan	172,742	25,155,064	$60,000	Tashkent	Uzbek and Russian
Vanuatu	4,710	192,910	$245	Port Vila	Bislama, English, and French
Vatican City (Holy See)	0	890	N/A	Vatican City	Italian
Venezuela	352,144	23,916,810	$146,200	Caracas	Spanish
Vietnam	127,244	79,939,014	$154,400	Hanoi	Vietnamese
Western Sahara	102,703	250,559	N/A	El Aaiun	Arabic, Spanish, and Hassani
Yemen	203,850	18,078,035	$14,400	Sanaá	Arabic
Zambia	290,586	9,770,199	$8,500	Lusaka	English and Bantu languages
Zimbabwe	150,804	11,365,366	$28,200	Harare	English, Shona, and Bantu languages

FACT! THE UNITED NATIONS was founded on October 24, 1945, as a successor to its failed predecessor the League of Nations. A single representative for each nation sits in the General Assembly, which can pass resolutions and adopt recommendations but has no power to impose its will on member states. The real power is the Security Council, which has five permanent members—the USA, China, Russia, the UK, and France—and ten temporary seats that are filled for two-year terms.

Arms and Armies

Biggest Armed Forces

The table below ranks the most powerful nations of the world in terms of the number of individuals serving in their armed forces.

Country	Size	Country	Size
China	2,810,000	South Korea	683,000
Russia	1,520,000 (NB: Many estimates of Russia's manpower place it at just over half this figure, knocking them down to 5th place)	Pakistan	612,000
		Turkey	610,000 (NB: Estimates of Turkey's military manpower vary between 500,000 and 700,000)
US	1,366,000	Iran	513,000
India	1,303,000	Vietnam	484,000
North Korea	1,000,000		

Most Powerful Navies

The figures here are for the number of ships and the total tonnage of fleets. The Combat Value includes personnel and preparedness.

Nation	Combat value	Number of ships	Thousands of tonnes
US	302	201	3,024
UK	46	102	510
Russia	45	187	908
Japan	26	124	310
China	16	219	346
France	14	43	197
India	10	57	164
Taiwan	10	68	140
Germany	9	110	120
Italy	9	99	140

Largest Airforces

Nation	Number of aircraft	Personnel	Nation	Number of aircraft	Personnel
US	2,000	590,000	France	850	90,000
Russia	2,100	130,000	UK	550	70,000
China	4,500	470,000	Germany	500	75,000
Ukraine	850	150,000	Israel	450	32,000
India	850	110,000	Italy	300	20,000

Countries with the Most Nuclear Warheads

Country	Number of warheads	Country	Number of warheads
Russia	28,240	UK	400
US	12,070	Israel	uncertain
France	510	India	uncertain
China	425	Pakistan	uncertain

Countries with the Largest Oil Reserves

Country	Barrels (billion)	Country	Barrels (billion)
Saudi Arabia	264.2	Russia	48.6
United Arab Emirates	97.8	Libya	29.5
Iran	89.7		

Where Would You Choose to Live?

Countries with the Best Quality of Life

Country	HDI*	Country	HDI*
Norway	0.942	United States	0.939
Sweden	0.941	Iceland	0.936
Canada	0.940	Netherlands	0.935
Australia	0.939	Japan	0.933
Belgium	0.939	Finland	0.930

* Countries rated using the Human Development Index (max. possible score = 1).

Most Dangerous Countries

Country	Risk rating and cause	Country	Risk rating and cause
Afghanistan	5/5 Armed militia	Chechnya	4/5 War zone
Congo	5/5 Civil war	Pakistan	4/5 Terrorism
Iraq	5/5 Damaged infrastructure	Solomon Islands	3/5 Political tension
Colombia	4/5 Drug trafficking	Liberia	3/5 Civil war
Yemen	4/5 Terrorism	Israel	3/5 Suicide bombings

Crime

Country	Crimes reported (most recent year)	Country	Crimes reported (most recent year)
US	23,677,800	Russia	2,952,367
Germany	6,264,723	Canada	2,476,520
UK	5,170,831	Japan	2,443,470
France	3,771,849	Italy	2,205,782
South Africa	3,422,743	India	1,764,629

Total number of crimes reported globally—70 million.

PLANTS AND
ANIMALS

The Kingdom of Living Things

Scientists classify living things according to a hierarchical system of categories, or taxa, often referred to as the Linnaean System after the man who initiated the system, the 18th-century Swedish naturalist Karl von Linné (the Latinized version of his name is *Carrolus Linnaeus*). The main taxa, in descending order of specificity, and using the example of humans, are:

Kingdom	*Animalia*				
Phylum	*Chordata*				
Subphylum	*Vertebrata*				
Class	*Mammalia*	*Pisces*	*Amphibia*	*Reptilia*	*Aves*
Order	*Primates*				
Family	*Hominidae*				
Genus	*Homo*				
Species	*Sapiens*				

Species

Total number of species known to science: *1,750,000.*
Proportion of which are insects: *two-thirds.*
Total number of species thought to exist: *between 10 and 100 million (probably about 14 million).*
Percentage of species that have existed, and which are already extinct: *99%.*
Percentage of species that are smaller than a bumblebee: *99%.*

Linnaeus believed that there were only two kingdoms—plants and animals. Today scientists distinguish between at least five different kingdoms, as detailed in the table below.

Kingdom	Structural organization	Method of nutrition	Types of organisms	Named species	Total species (estimate)
Monera	Small, simple single cells called prokaryotes (in which nucleus is not enclosed by a membrane); some form chains or mats	Absorb food	Bacteria, blue-green algae, and spirochetes	4,000	1,000,000
Protista	Large, single cells, called eukaryotes (in which nucleus is enclosed by a membrane); some form chains or colonies	Absorb, ingest, and /or photo-synthesize food	Protozoans and algae of various types	80,000	600,000
Fungi	Multicellular filamentous forms with specialized eukaryotic cells	Absorb food	Fungi, molds, mushrooms, yeasts, mildews, and smuts	72,000	1,500,000
Plantae	Multicellular forms with specialized eukaryotic cells; do not have their own means of locomotion	Photo-synthesize food	Mosses, ferns, woody and non-woody flowering plants	270,000	320,000
Animalia	Multicellular forms with specialized eukaryotic cells; have their own means of locomotion	Ingest food	Sponges, worms, insects, fish, amphibians, reptiles, birds, and mammals	1,326,239	9,812,298

Collective Nouns for Animals

There is a great diversity of collective nouns denoting groups of animals—a "quiver" of cobras, a "murder" of crows, and a "tribe"

Animal name	Collective noun	Animal name	Collective noun
Apes	Shrewdness	Dolphins	Pod
Asses	Pace	Doves	Dule, pitying (specific to turtle doves)
Badgers	Cete	Ducks	Brace, flock (in flight), raft, paddling (on water), team
Bats	Colony		
Bears	Sloth, sleuth, pack		
Beavers	Colony, lodge	Eagles	Convocation
Bees	Grist, hive, flight, swarm	Elephants	Herd
		Elk	Gang
Birds in general	Flight (in the air), flock (on the ground)	Finches	Charm
		Fish	Draught, nest, school, shoal
Buzzards	Wake		
Caterpillars	Army	Foxes	Leash, skulk, earth
Cats	Clowder, pounce (for kittens—kindle, litter, intrigue)	Frogs	Army
		Game Birds	Volary, brace (referring to a pair or couple killed by a hunter)
Cattle	Drove, herd, yoke (pair), team, kine		
Clams	Bed	Geese	Flock, gaggle (on the ground), skein/wedge (in flight)
Cockroaches	Intrusion		
Cobras	Quiver	Giraffes	Tower, corps, herd
Cormorants	Gulp	Gnats	Cloud, horde
Crocodiles	Bask, float, congregation	Goats	Tribe, trip
		Gorillas	Band
Crows	Murder	Gulls	Colony
Deer	Herd, parcel, bevy (refers only to roe deer)	Hawks	Cast, kettle (flying in large numbers), boil (two or more spiraling in flight)
Dogs (see also Hounds)	Litter (young), pack (wild)		

of goats. The English language is particularly rich in these strange and unusual terms. Below is a list of correct terms for describing groups of animals—some less well-known than others.

Animal name	Collective noun	Animal name	Collective noun
Hippo- potamuses	Bloat, crash, herd, thunder	Peacocks	Muster, ostentation
		Penguins	Colony
Hornets	Nest	Pigs	Drift, drove, litter (young), sounder (of swine), team, passel (of hogs)
Horses	Team, harras, rag (for colts), stud (group of horses belonging to a single owner), string (ponies)		
		Quails	Bevy, covey
Hounds	Cry, mute, pack, kennel	Rabbits	Colony, warren, nest, herd (domestic only), litter (young)
Hyenas	Cackle	Rats	Colony, horde, pack, plague, swarm
Jays	Party, scold		
Jellyfish	Smack	Ravens	Unkindness
Kangaroos	Mob, troop	Seals	Pod, herd, colony
Lapwings	Deceit	Sharks	Shiver
Larks	Ascension, exaltation	Sheep	Drove, flock, herd
Leopards	Leap, lepe	Snakes, vipers	Nest
Lions	Pride	Snipes	Walk, wisp
Locusts	Plague	Sparrows	Host
Magpies	Tiding, murder	Squirrels	Dray, scurry
Martens	Richness	Starlings	Murmuration
Moles	Labour	Storks	Muster
Monkeys	Tribe, troop	Tigers	Streak
Nightingales	Watch	Toads	Knot
Otters	Romp, family	Trout	Hover
Owls	Parliament	Turtles	Bale
Oxen	Team, yoke, drove	Whales	Pod, gam, herd
Parrots	Company, prattle	Wolves	Pack, rout or route (when in movement)

Biggest Living Thing

The world's biggest living things are plant or fungal networks where many apparent individuals are actually clones of one another sharing the same root systems or mycelial (mass of interwoven) networks. An *Armillaria ostoyae* (honey mushroom) fungus growing in the Malheur National Forest in the Blue Mountains of Eastern Oregon covers nearly 2,220 acres (equivalent to about 1,220 soccer fields).

A grove of quaking aspens (*Populus tremuloides*) growing in the Wasatch Mountains, Utah, US—nicknamed Pando (meaning "I spread") by scientists—covers a smaller area (200 acres) but weighs in at 6,600 tons. Although it appears to be a forest, all of the trees actually stem from one enormous root system.

Oldest Living Thing

If you include clones, such as the quaking aspen grove described above, whereby new growths develop from previously existing plants or fungi, the oldest living things may be millions of years old.

Discounting other types of clone (for example, asexually reproducing amoebas or plants) and dormant spores from ancient tombs, the oldest living thing is Methuselah, an ancient bristlecone pine (*Pinus longaeva & aristata*) that is 4,767 years old—a millennium older than any other tree yet discovered. Methuselah lives in the White Mountains of California, although its exact location is a closely guarded secret to preserve it from vandals and trophy hunters.

Rarest living thing Lonesome George—the only surviving Abingdon Island giant tortoise.

Record-Breaking Plants

Biggest tree alive today: *General Sherman—a giant sequoia* (Sequoiadendron giganteum) *growing in the Sequoia National Park, California, is 275 ft tall.*

Biggest tree ever: *the Lindsey Creek tree, a coast redwood* (Sequoia sempervirens) *in California. It had a total trunk volume of 90,000 ft³ and a mass of 3,248 tonnes. The tree blew over in a storm in 1905.*

Biggest tree girth ever recorded: *this stood at 190 ft and was a European chestnut* (Castanea sativa) *called The Tree Of A Hundred Horses, on Mt Etna, Sicily, Italy, in 1780; it is now split into three separate parts.*

Longest roots: *a wild fig tree (genus* Ficus) *at Echo Caves, near Ohrigstad, Transvaal, South Africa, has roots that penetrate 393.7 ft deep. The winter rye,* Secale cereale, *can produce up to 387 miles of roots in 1.8 ft³ of earth.*

Largest seed: *the double coconut or coco de mer, fruit of the giant fan palm* (Lodoicea maldivica) *weighs up to 44 lb, also making it the world's biggest cell.*

Largest leaves: *the raffia palm* (Raphia farinifera) *of the Mascarene Islands, Indian Ocean, and the Amazonian bamboo palm* (Raphia taedigera), *of South America and Africa, have leaves that can grow up to 66 ft long, but these are divided into fronds or strands. The largest undivided leaves belong to the* Alocasia macrorrhiza, *from Sabah, Malaysia, an aquatic plant resembling a giant water lily. A specimen found in 1966 was 10 ft long, 6 ft 4 in wide, and had a surface area of 34 sq ft.*

Fastest-growing plant: *bamboo can grow as fast as 3 ft per day, a rate of 0.00002 mph. Bamboo grows one-third faster than the fastest-growing tree.*

Largest flower: *the orange, brown, and white parasite* Rafflesia arnoldi *has flowers measuring up to 3 ft across, weighing up to 24 lb.*

Largest forest: *the taiga—coniferous forest—of northern Russia covers a total area of 2.7 billion acres.*

Record-Breaking Animals

Biggest spider: *the Goliath bird-eating spider (*Theraphosa blondi*). In 1998 a two-year-old male specimen raised in Scotland had a leg span of 11 in—as big as a dinner plate—and weighed 6 oz.*

Biggest amphibian: *the Chinese giant salamander (*Andrias davidianus*). A specimen caught in Hunan Province was 5 ft 11 in long.*

Biggest crocodile: *estuarine or saltwater crocodile (*Crocodylus porosus*). A specimen at the Bhitarkanika Wildlife Sanctuary in Orissa State, India, is over 23 ft long, but there are reports of wild crocodiles growing to lengths of over 33 ft.*

Longest snake: *reticulated python (*Python reticulates*)—a specimen shot in Celebes, Indonesia, in 1912, was 33 ft long.*

Biggest fish: *the whale shark (*Rhincodon typus*)—the biggest recorded specimen was 41 ft 6 in long.*

Biggest living bird: *the ostrich—up to 9 ft tall, and weighing 345 lb.*

Biggest wingspan: *male wandering albatross (*Diomedea exulans*)— from tip to tip, its wings measure 11 ft 11 in.*

Biggest-ever flying creature: *the pterosaur (*Quetzalcoatlus northropi*) had a wingspan of 36–39 ft. Became extinct 70 million years ago.*

Largest land mammal: *male African bush elephant (*Loxodonta africana*). The largest specimen ever recorded was shot in Mucusso, Angola, on November 7, 1974; it had a standing height of about 13 ft and weighed over 12 tonnes.*

Tallest mammal: *the giraffe (*Giraffa camelopardalis*). The tallest specimen ever recorded ("George" of Chester Zoo, England) was 19 ft tall.*

Largest mammal: *the blue whale (*Balaenoptera musculus*) can grow to a length of 115 ft and weigh up to 130 tonnes, making it the largest animal ever to have lived.*

Loudest animal: *blue whales make low-frequency sounds that are louder than a jet engine—up to 188 decibels (dB).*

Oldest animal: *a Madagascar radiated tortoise (*Astrochelys radiata*), called Tui Malila, lived to be at least 188. It was presented to the explorer Captain Cook in the 1770s and died in 1965.*

Speed Records

Bird: *the peregrine falcon* (Falco peregrinus) *can reach speeds of up to 217 mph as it dives.*

Fish: *the cosmopolitan sailfish* (Istiophorus platypterus) *has been recorded as having reached a speed of 68 mph.*

Mammal: *the cheetah* (Acinonyx jubatus) *can run at 60 mph in short bursts. The pronghorn or American antelope* (Antilocapra americana) *can maintain 55 mph over half a mile.*

Land bird: *the ostrich* (Struthio camelus) *can sprint at up to 45 mph.*

Slowest mammal: *the three-toed sloth* (Bradypus tridactylus) *of South America has an average ground speed of 0.1 mph.*

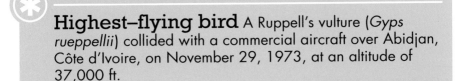

Highest–flying bird A Ruppell's vulture (*Gyps rueppellii*) collided with a commercial aircraft over Abidjan, Côte d'Ivoire, on November 29, 1973, at an altitude of 37,000 ft.

Dangerous Animals

The "animal" that has killed the most people is probably the malarial parasite *Plasmodium*, thought to have been responsible for half of all natural deaths since the Stone Age. Apart from disease organisms, the most dangerous animals are probably the housefly and the mosquito, which spread illnesses such as dysentery and malaria—and last, but not least, humans themselves.

Most Dangerous Small Animals

Bees and wasps: *kill more people than any other small creature, thanks to anaphylaxis (allergic reactions). Range: worldwide.*

Australian sea wasp, or box jellyfish (*Chironex fleckeri*): *the most poisonous creature in the world. Each one contains enough poison to kill 60 humans in as little as four minutes.*

Stonefish (*Synanceja horrida*): *most venomous fish in the world. Found in Indo-Pacific. No fewer than 13 spines on its back, which inject poison into the foot if stepped on. Death occurs within six hours.*

Sydney funnel web spider (*Atrax robustus*): *although its venom is not as toxic as the Sicarius spider from southern Africa, the funnel web spider is much more common and much more aggressive.*

Most Dangerous Big Animals

Small animals like insects and snakes may kill the most people, but it's the big ones that are the most dangerous in a one-on-one situation. Here are the top three most dangerous big animals in the world:

Buffalo: *the African or Cape buffalo is aggressive, incredibly strong, and very fast. These buffaloes are thought to account for several hundred lives lost in Africa each year, although figures are hard to come by because few records are kept in the regions where they tend to attack.*

Crocodiles and alligators: *although saltwater or estuarine crocodiles are big and aggressive, they generally account for only one death per year. The Nile Crocodile kills the most humans—probably over a hundred a year.*

Polar bear: *the world's largest land predator, the polar bear is particularly dangerous because it will actively hunt humans.*

THE
HUMAN
BODY

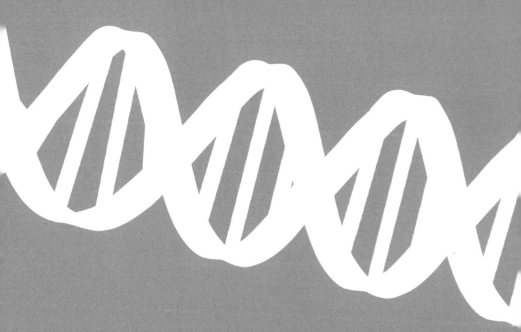

The Amazing Human Body

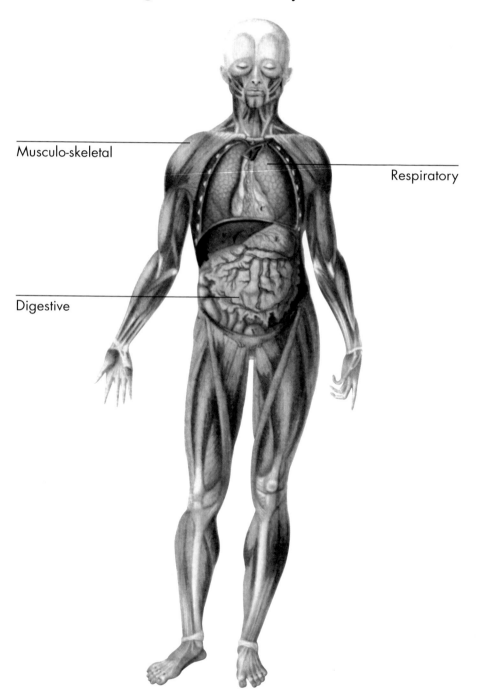

Musculo-skeletal

Respiratory

Digestive

There are nine major systems in the human body:

Digestive

Processes food to release and absorb nutrients; houses symbiotic bacteria that generate important nutrients; processes toxins and disposes of waste products. **Major components:** *digestive tract, stomach, liver, pancreas, gallbladder, teeth, tongue.*

> **Length of digestive tract:** *26 ft.*
> *Stomach acid is 1,600 times more acidic than vinegar.*
> **Number of bacteria in your gut:** *750 trillion.*
> **Number of cells in your entire body:** *75 trillion.*
> **Time spent eating and drinking in average lifespan:** *5 years.*
> **Average time for a meal to transit from mouth to rectum:** *14–24 hours.*

Musculo-skeletal

Supports and moves body; protects internal systems. **Major components:** *bones, muscles, joints, tendons, ligaments, cartilage.*

- *Human bone is as strong as iron, but three times lighter.*
- *85 percent of your body heat is produced by muscle contraction.*
- *The jaw muscles used for chewing are strong enough to support your entire body weight.*
- *Between 10 and 30 percent of the adult skeleton is replenished each year.*
- *You are literally not the same person you were two years ago—almost every cell in your body has died and been replaced with a new one.*

Nervous

Controls and coordinates other body systems using electrochemical pathways; plans and executes responses; seat of consciousness, drives, and emotions. **Major components:** *brain, sense organs, spinal cord, nerves.*

Respiratory

Oxygenates blood and expels waste carbon dioxide; helps regulate heat and moisture; important for sound, speech, smell. **Major components:** *lungs, trachea, bronchi, vocal cords, sinuses, nose.*

Cardiovascular

Circulates blood around the body, carrying oxygen to tissues and removing waste; helps repair wounds. **Major components:** *heart, arteries, veins and capillaries, blood, bone marrow.*

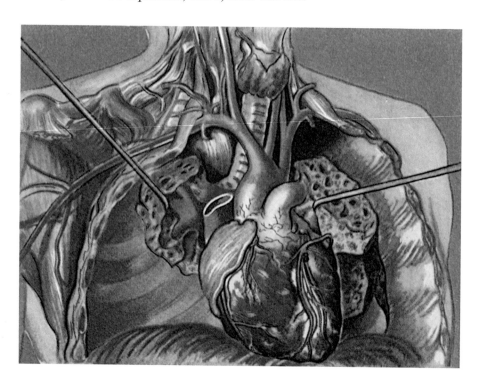

Immuno–lymphatic

Protects against threats to health; helps dispose of waste and maintain fluid balance in tissues. **Major components:** *lymph vessels and nodes, immune cells in blood, spleen, thymus, skin.*

- *You have between 10.6 and 12.7 pints of blood flowing through your circulatory system if you're a man, and 8.5 and 10.6 pints if you're a woman.*
- *One drop of blood contains over 250 million cells.*
- *The total surface area of all the red blood cells in an average adult is around 4,545 sq yards—enough to cover four tennis courts.*
- *An average red blood cell lives for only 120 days, during which time it will travel 300 miles on its journey round and round the body.*

Endocrine

Hormonal control and coordination system; oversees growth cycles; modulates emotions and sensations; involved in digestion, reproduction, immune function, milk production, thermoregulation. **Major components:** *hypothalamus, pituitary gland, thymus, pancreas, liver, adrenal glands, breasts, sex organs, sweat glands.*

Urinary

Disposes of waste products, maintains fluid balance. **Major components:** *kidneys, bladder, urethra.*

- *The kidneys process around 40 gallons of fluid a day to produce around 1.75 pints of urine a day.*
- *Your kidneys process 600 times their own weight of fluid every day.*
- *A typical red blood cell travels through your kidneys 360 times a day.*
- *The entire blood supply of your body passes through your kidneys roughly once every four minutes.*
- *About 30 percent of people have an accessory renal artery—an extra artery supplying blood to the kidneys.*
- *In a normal adult, the bladder rarely holds more than 10.8 fl oz of urine, with the urge to urinate coming at the 9.5 fl oz mark. Over 16.9 fl oz causes pain and an intense urge to urinate immediately.*
- *Urine gets its color from a nitrogen-containing pigment called urochrome.*

Reproductive

Produces and delivers gametes; houses and nurtures fetus/embryo. **Major components:** *testes/ovaries, penis/vagina, uterus/prostate gland, reproductive tracts.*

- *A female fetus carries 7 million egg cells in her proto-ovaries. All but 400,000 of these will have died by the time she reaches puberty.*
- *A single male ejaculation contains 200 million sperm—enough to generate the combined populations of Britain, France, and Germany.*
- *A human sperm leaving the penis travels at 8,000 body lengths per second, equivalent to a human swimming at 34,000 mph.*

DNA and the Human Genome

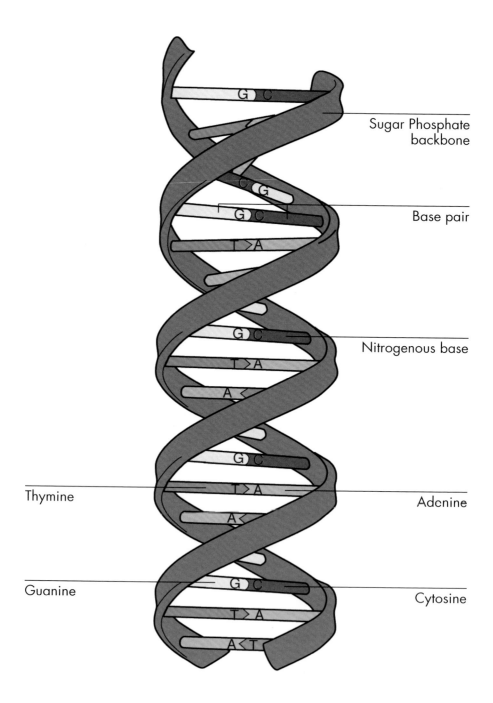

Sugar Phosphate backbone

Base pair

Nitrogenous base

Thymine

Adenine

Guanine

Cytosine

Structure of DNA

Deoxyribonucleic acid (DNA) is structured like a ladder made of two strands that join in the middle. The sides of the ladder are formed by strings of sugar and phosphate molecules. The rungs are formed by pairs of compounds, called "bases," which come in four varieties, two small, and two large. Each rung is made up of one large base joined to one small base. The two large bases are A (adenine) and G (guanine); the two small bases are C (cytosine) and T (thymine). The shapes of the bases are complementary, so that they always join in the same way—thus A fits only with T, and G fits only with C.

DNA Dimensions

Width of DNA molecule: *79 billionths of an inch.*
Total length of DNA in a single cell: *3 feet.*
Number of times the DNA in your body would stretch to the Sun and back if put end to end: *over 600.*

Comparative Genomes

The genome is the total package that makes up an organism's genetic blueprint. As geneticists have probed the genomes of more and more organisms, they have arrived at some surprising discoveries about the relative size and apparent complexity of different creatures—and about how many of our genes appear in other creatures.

Number of genes in human genome: *32,000.*
Number of genes in fruit-fly genome: *13,600.*
Percentage similarity between human genome and that of . . .
  Dogs: *85 percent.*
  Chimpanzees: *98 percent (higher than between chimps and gorillas).*
Length of human genome: *3 billion base-pairs.*
Length of salamander genome: *60 billion base-pairs.*
Length of field-lily genome: *100 billion base-pairs.*
Number of known human disease genes: *289.*
Number of human disease genes with direct counterparts in fruit-fly genome: *177.*

Human Genome Project

The Human Genome Project was an international collaboration set up to determine the complete sequence of the three billion DNA subunits (bases) of the human genome, and to identify all human genes, to make these accessible for biological study. The genomes of several other organisms were sequenced for comparative purposes.

Cloning

A clone is an organism that is genetically identical to another organism. Identical twins are natural clones, as are strawberry plants that reproduce by sending out runners. Cloning is the process of creating a clone—usually an animal clone—by artificial means.

Time Scale of Cloning

See the table below for a list of cloning milestones, from the tentative early steps well over a hundred years ago, to the major breakthroughs of the 20th century.

Year	Milestone	What was created?
1891	First artificial clone of an animal	Sea urchin—created by Hans Driesch in Naples, Italy
1902	First artificial clone of a vertebrate	Salamander—created by Hans Spemann in Würzburg, Germany
1951	First clone using nuclear transfer	Frog—created by team of Robert Briggs, Philadelphia, US
1993	First cloned human embryo	At George Washington University, Washington, DC, US
1996	First clone from an adult cell	Dolly the Sheep—at the Roslin Institute, Scotland, UK
2001	First cloned pet	Tabby cat—by Genetics Savings and Clone, US

Bones in the Adult Human Body

Total number of bones: *newborn babies have over 300 bones, but many of these then fuse together; by adulthood, the average human body has precisely 206 bones.*

Longest bone: *femur (quarter of total body length).*

Shortest bone: *stapes (stirrup bone in inner ear), measuring 0.1 in.*

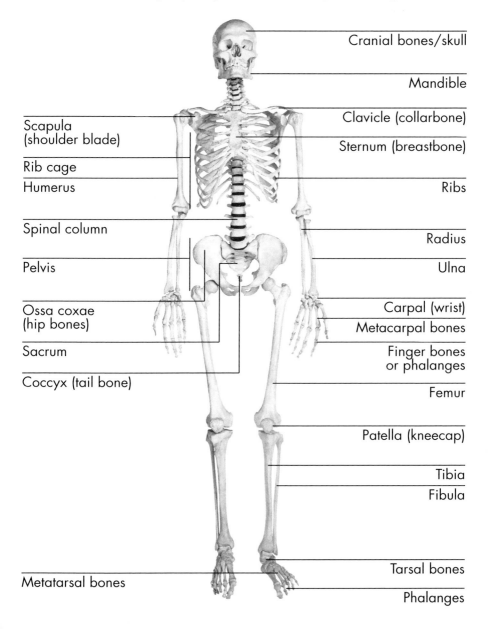

Cranial bones/skull

Mandible

Clavicle (collarbone)

Sternum (breastbone)

Ribs

Radius

Ulna

Carpal (wrist)

Metacarpal bones

Finger bones or phalanges

Femur

Patella (kneecap)

Tibia

Fibula

Tarsal bones

Phalanges

Scapula (shoulder blade)

Rib cage

Humerus

Spinal column

Pelvis

Ossa coxae (hip bones)

Sacrum

Coccyx (tail bone)

Metatarsal bones

The Human Brain

There are four divisions of the brain. They are: the brainstem, which includes the medulla, midbrain, and reticular formation; the cerebellum; the limbic system (subdivided into the thalamus, hypothalamus, mamillary body, olfactory lobe, hippocampus, amygdala, fornix, and septum pellucidum); and the cerebrum (subdivided into cerebral hemispheres and lobes).

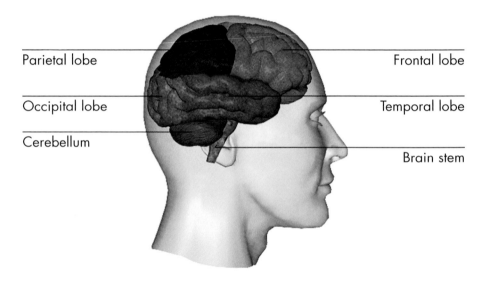

Parietal lobe

Occipital lobe

Cerebellum

Frontal lobe

Temporal lobe

Brain stem

Lobe	Mainly concerned with	Lobe	Mainly concerned with
Occipital	Vision	Parietal	Sensation
Temporal	Smell, hearing, language	Frontal	Movement, planning, reason

Brain statistics (figures are for an "average" brain)

Width: *5.5 in.*
Length: *6.6 in.*
Height: *3.7 in.*
Weight of human brain: *3 lb.*
Weight of elephant brain: *14 lb.*

Weight of cat brain: *0.7 lb.*
Total surface area of human cortex: *~2.5 sq ft.*
Number of neurons (nerve cells) in human brain: *100 billion.*
Number of neurons in octopus brain: *300 million.*
Number of connections between neurons: *100 trillion (more than the number of leaves on trees in the Amazon rainforest).*
Rate of loss of brain cells in average adult: *100,000 per day.*
Proportion of brain lost over course of life: *7 percent.*
Maximum traveling speed of a nervous impulse: *270 mph.*

In theory, the human brain has the ability to store more memories than there are atoms in the universe.

Mind over matter Hindu holy men, known as *saddhus*, can consciously slow their heart rate to just two beats a minute. They are also able to remain under water for up to six minutes.

Some Tibetan monks practice a skill known as *tumo*, whereby they learn to raise the temperature of their fingers and toes by up to 15°F, simply by sheer effort of will.

The world record for time spent without sleep is 264 hours (11 days), set by Randy Gardner in 1965.

IQ Scale

Scale	Level	Scale	Level
130+	Very Superior	69 and below	Mental Retardation
120–129	Superior		
110–119	High Average	55–69	Mild Retardation
90–109	Average	40–54	Moderate Retardation
80–89	Low Average	25–39	Severe Retardation
70–79	Borderline Mental Retardation	–25	Profound Retardation

Super Senses

Hearing

Range of human hearing: *20 to 20,000 Hz.*
Minimum range of pigeon hearing: *0.1 Hz.*
Range of elephant hearing: *1 to 20,000 Hz.*
Range of mouse hearing: *1,000 to 100,000 Hz.*
Range of noctuid moth hearing: *1,000 to 240,000 Hz.*
Upper limit of bat hearing: *250,000 Hz.*
Maximum resolution of bat hearing (echolocation): *0.25 mm; width of a human hair.*
Pain threshold for noise: *130 dB.*
Damage threshold for noise: *90 dB.*
Noise level of a quiet room at night: *20 dB.*
Noise level of ordinary conversation: *60 dB.*
Noise level of loud bar/restaurant: *90 dB.*
Noise level of typical construction project: *110 dB.*

Taste

Primary taste sensations: *salt, sweet, sour, bitter.*
Number of human taste buds (incl. tongue, palate, cheeks): *10,000. The human tongue can taste 1 teaspoon of sugar in 19 pints of water.*
Number of taste buds in pig tongue: *15,000.*
Number of taste buds in rabbit tongue: *17,000.*
Number of taste buds in catfish tongue: *100,000.*
Concentration of fish extract detectable by shark: *one part in 10 billion.*

Smell

Number of human olfactory receptor cells: *40 million.*
Number of separate odors average person can recognize: *10,000.*

Number of males that can be attracted by a single female Bombay moth: *1 million trillion males.*

Distance from which a silkworm moth can detect another moth: *7 miles.*

Concentration of pheromone that a silkworm moth can detect: *1 molecule of pheromone per 10^{17} molecules of air.*

Age of scent trail that bloodhound can follow: *four days. The membrane in the bloodhound's nose that detects odors is 50 times bigger and a million times more sensitive than a human's.*

Vision

Number of photoreceptors in human retina: *105 million.*

Maximum density of photoreceptors in human retina: *200,000 per sq mm.*

Flicker fusion rate (max. number of distinguishable frames) in bright light: *60/sec.*

Flicker fusion rate in dim light: *24/sec.*

Fusion flicker rate of fly: *300/sec.*

Max resolution of human vision: *100 microns.*

Max resolution of the butterfly *Colias*: *30 microns.*

Distance at which a single candle can be detected by the human eye in ideal (i.e. dark) conditions: *30 miles.*

Distance from which a falcon can see a 4-in object: *0.93 miles.*

Height from which a buzzard can spot a mouse: *15,000 ft.*

Visible spectrum: *370–730 nanometers (nm).*

Touch

Number of touch receptors in human hand: *17,000. The star-nosed mole has six times more touch receptors in its nose than does a human hand.*

Height from which a bee's wing can be dropped and its impact felt on human face: *0.39 in.*

Human skin can detect a temperature change of 1.8°F.

Leading Causes of World Mortality

Cause	Total deaths (in thousands)	Percentage of total
Heart attack (ischaemic heart disease)	7,181	12.7
Stroke (cerebrovascular disease)	5,454	9.6
Lower respiratory infections	3,871	6.8
HIV/AIDS	2,866	5.1
Chronic obstructive pulmonary disease	2,672	4.7
Diarrheal diseases	2,001	3.5
Tuberculosis	1,644	2.9
Childhood diseases	1,318	2.3
Cancer of trachea/bronchus/lung	1,213	2.1
Road traffic accidents	1,194	2.1%
Malaria	1,124	2.0
High blood pressure (hypertensive heart disease)	874	1.5
Other unintentional injuries	874	1.5
Stomach cancer	850	1.5
Suicide	849	1.5
Cirrhosis of the liver	796	1.4
Measles	745	1.3
Kidney disease (nephritis/nephrosis)	625	1.1
Liver cancer	616	1.1
Colon/rectal cancer	615	1.1

HUMAN
ENDEAVOR

Great Achievements in Engineering

The chart below gives the 20 greatest engineering achievements of the modern era, according to a poll of 60 engineering societies conducted by the US National Academy of Engineering.

Rank	Achievement	Rank	Achievement
1	Electrification	11	Highways
2	Automobile	12	Spacecraft
3	Airplane	13	Internet
4	Water supply and distribution	14	Imaging
5	Electronics	15	Household appliances
6	Radio and television	16	Health technologies
7	Agricultural mechanization	17	Petroleum and petrochemical technologies
8	Computers		
9	Telephone	18	Laser and fiber optics
10	Air conditioning and refrigeration	19	Nuclear technologies
		20	High-performance materials

World's Greatest Dams

There are two basic types of dam. The gravity dam uses sheer weight of material to hold back the water behind it, while the arch dam uses an arc shape to redirect the pressure of water into the sides of a valley.

There are more than 40,000 large dams (defined as being those more than 16 yards in height) and 800,000 small ones worldwide. Together, they generate 19 percent of the world's electricity, and irrigate 16 percent of the world's food supply.

Three Gorges Dam, China

The world's greatest dam but one that forced between 40 and 80 million people to leave their homes. The reservoir is larger than Lake Superior.

Completion: *2008.*
Width: *1 mile.*
Height: *600 ft.*
Reservoir capacity: *1.39 trillion cubic feet.*
Generating capacity: *18,000 megawatts (MW).*

Itaipú Dam, Brazil/Paraguay
Currently the world's most powerful dam, generating 12,700 megawatts of electricity.
Completion: *1991.*
Reservoir capacity: *1.02 trillion cubic feet.*
Generating capacity: *12,600 megawatts (MW).*

World's Longest Bridges

When completed, the projected bridge across the Messina Straits between the Mediterranean island of Sicily and the Italian mainland will have a central span of 10,824 ft.

Longest in total length: *23.9 miles—Second Lake Pontchartrain Causeway, from Mandeville to Metairie, Louisiana, US. Opened: 1969.*
Longest span: *6,530 ft—Akashi-Kaikyo Bridge, from Kobe to Naruto, Japan. Opened: 1998.*

FACT! One of the world's highest dams is the Verzasca Dam in Switzerland (completed in 1965), the location for a record-breaking bungee jump that has been voted as the greatest stunt of all time. The jump featured in the opening sequence of the 1995 James Bond movie *Goldeneye.* Stuntman Wayne Michaels plunged 750 ft down the front of the dam – a new world record for a bungee jump from a fixed object. Voters in a Sky Movies Poll chose the stunt ahead of classics from *Ben Hur* and *Indiana Jones.*

World's Tallest Buildings

The winner of the coveted title depends on the definition. The tallest free-standing structure in the world is currently the CN Tower in Toronto (opened 1976), which measures 1,815 ft. But the structure does not meet the standard definition of a building as being primarily for human habitation (with the greatest majority of its height divided into occupiable floors). If a building meets this definition, its height is measured from ground level—at the main entrance—to the structural apex of the building. This includes spires but does not include television antennae, radio antennae, or flagpoles.

Building and location	Height (feet)	Floors	Year completed	Architect
Center of India Tower, Katangi, India	2,222	224	2016 (projected)	Undisclosed consortium
MTR Tower (Kowloon Station), Hong Kong	1,883	102	cancelled	Skidmore, Owings and Merrill
Freedom Tower, NYC (WTC replacement)	1,776	104	2014	Daniel Libeskind
Shanghai World Financial Center, China	1,509	95+	2004	Kohn Pedersen Fox Associates
Petronas Towers, Kuala Lumpur, Malaysia	1,483	88	1998	Cesar Pelli
Sears Tower, Chicago, US	1,450	110	1974	Bruce Graham
Jin Mao Building, Shanghai	1,381	88	1999	Skidmore, Owings and Merrill

FACT! The Empire State Building went from drawing board to finished article in just 20 months. At one point, there were 3,500 workers on the site, and the building was rising at the rate of one story per day.

Past and Present Record Holders

Petronas Towers 1998

Sears Tower 1974

World Trade Center 1971

Empire State Building 1931

Chrysler Building 1930

Manhattan Company 1930

Woolworth Building 1913

Metropolitan Life Tower 1909

Singer Building 1908

Park Row Building 1899

St Paul Building 1898

Manhattan Life 1894

Masonic Temple 1892

World Building 1890

1600 1400 1200 1000 800 600 400 200

Cultural Timeline

This timeline presents a partial overview of milestones in world cultural development from 30,000 BCE to the turn of the 20th century.

Year	Period	Development
30,000–8000 BCE	Prehistoric	Venus figures (30–15,000 BCE), cave paintings (20–10,000 BCE); few artifacts survive
8000–3000	River Valley civilizations	Monumental sculpture and architecture, murals and friezes in Mesopotamia; earliest written music; invention of writing
3000–1500	Nilotic and Asian civilizations	Monumental sculpture and architecture (pyramids, Sphinx), murals and friezes in Egypt – also harps and flutes developed; *Epic of Gilgamesh*; Vedic age in India (composition of religious epics)
1900–1100	Minoan and Mycenean periods; Shang Dynasty	Sophisticated painting, music, dance, and artisans; composition of Old Testament; beginning of Chinese literature
800–500	Archaic and Etruscan periods; Zhou Dynasty	Assyrian architecture and murals; Homeric epics; Black Figure vases; Doric order; Etruscan murals and bronzes; Pythagoras introduces the octave; Five Classics in China
500–300	Classical (Hellenic) period	Red-figure vases; Elgin Marbles; Acropolis, Parthenon; Ionic order; development of comedy and tragedy; Buddhist art and literature in India; Classical Chinese philosophy
300 BCE–150 CE	Hellenistic and Graeco-Roman periods; Qin and Han dynasties	Library of Alexandria; Corinthian order; Olympieium; mosaics and murals; Pantheon and Colosseum in Rome; *Bhagavad Gita*, Pankrits in India; Confucian classics in China
100–500	Early Christian and Early Byzantine; Celtic; Hindu Renaissance; Time of Troubles in China	Craftsmanship and jewelry; book illumination; painting and murals in Byzantium; hymns and church choral music; Taoist and Buddhist art and literature in China

Year	Period	Development
500–1000	Dark Ages; Byzantine; Islamic; Sui and Tang Dynasties	Romanesque architecture; book illumination; first polyphonic music; composition of Koran; Islamic architecture (Dome of the Rock); early Muslim art and vernacular literature in India; popular literature in China; Nara literature in Japan
1000–1400	Middle Ages; Song Dynasty; Heian and Kamakura period in Japan; Mandingo	Gothic architecture, stained glass; Giotto frescoes; Petrarch, Bocaccio, Chaucer, Dante; troubadour music, ballads, romances; New Confucian and prose style in China; Tale of Genjii and Kamakura poetry in Japan; W African Mandingo culture reaches height
1400–1600	Renaissance; Mughal period in India; Muromachi period in Japan; Songhay and Benin	Gutenberg Bible; Cervantes, Shakespeare; use of perspective in art; Da Vinci, Michelangelo, Durer, Raphael, Titian; Mannerism in Italy; Bhakti literature in India; Noh theatre in Japan; W African Songhay and Benin cultures reach heights (bronzework)
1550–1700	Baroque; Qing dynasty in China; Tokugawa period in Japan	Baroque style; Caravaggio, Poussin, Old Masters, Night Watch (Rembrandt); Monteverdi, Vivaldi, Bach, Handel; beginning of opera and ballet, first women in plays; Beijing Opera; Kabuki and Floating World arts in Japan
1700–1800	Rococo and Classical; Colonial period in India	Neo-classical and Rococo style; Birth of the novel; Voltaire, Rousseau; Goya; Haydn, Mozart
1800–1850	Romantic	Caspar David Friedrich; Byron, Wordsworth, Shelley, Coleridge, Schiller, Hugo; Beethoven, Chopin; invention of photography; new literary movements in China
1850–1900	Late Romantic, realism and impressionism; Meiji era in Japan; Colonial period Africa	Gothic revival, Pre-Raphaelites, Arts and Crafts, Art Nouveau; Van Gogh, Monet, Renoir, Rodin, Cezanne; Liszt, Verdi, Wagner, Tchaikovsky; Whitman, Emerson, Dostoyevsky, Tolstoy, Dickens, Conrad; first haute couture fashion house; birth of cinema; birth of the skyscraper; birth of ragtime; Meiji literature, Haiku poetry

20th Century Cultural Timeline

Key cultural milestones for the 20th century, from 1900 to the turn of the millennium.

Year	Period	Development
1900–1920	Modernism, expressionism, cubism, abstract and conceptual art	Art Deco, Fauvism, Dadaism; Picasso (Blue, Rose and Cubist periods), Matisse, Duchamp, Kandinsky; Joyce, Chekhov, Bloomsbury Group, Virgina Woolf; science fiction and pulp fiction; method acting, realism; birth of Hollywood, *Great Train Robbery*, DW Griffiths *Birth of a Nation*, Chaplin; Debussy, Mahler, Stravinsky *Firebird*; first popular music chart; development of jazz; modern dance (Isadora Duncan, Diaghilev); Coco Chanel
1920–1930	Surrealism, Jazz Age	Surrealism, neoplasticism, Bauhaus, Prairie Style (Frank Lloyd Wright); Dali; Harlem Renaissance; Walt Disney, Eisenstein *Battleship Potemkin*, first talkie – *The Jazz Singer*; first commercial radio broadcasts, invention of TV; Woody Guthrie, Louis Armstrong, Jelly Roll Morton; Ravel *Bolero*, Gershwin *Rhapsody in Blue*; flappers
1930–1940	Depression era	Picasso (Guernica); Cartier-Bresson; Golden Age of Hollywood, *Gone With the Wind*, *Wizard of Oz*; BBC broadcasts first television service, Welles *War of the Worlds*; introduction of the paperback; Swing music, Duke Ellington
1940–1950	Post-war era	International style in architecture; abstract expressionism, Henry Moore; Hemingway *For Whom the Bell Tolls*, Tennessee Williams *A Streetcar Named Desire*; film noir, Welles *Citizen Kane*, neorealism in Italy; first TV soap; Britten *Peter Grimes*, Rodgers and Hammerstein *Oklahoma!*; Dior's New Look
1950–1960	Rock'n'roll era	Action paintings, Jackson Pollock, Color-field painting, Rothko; Angry Young Men, John Osborne, Kingsley Amis, William Golding *Lord of the Flies*; birth of rock 'n'roll, Elvis first rock star, Bernstein *West*

Year	Period	Development
		Side Story, Sinatra *Come Dance With Me*; growing popularity of TV
1960–1970	Swinging Sixties	Pop art, op art; Warhol, Lichtenstein, Bridget Riley; *Psycho*, *Sound of Music*, *Midnight Cowboy*, New Wave in France; *Sesame Street*; Philip Roth; *Rolling Stone* magazine; New Wave jazz (Coltrane), Beatlemania, Woodstock, Bob Dylan, Rolling Stones, mods; Pierre Cardin – first licences, first ready-to-wear, Quant – mini-skirt, Calvin Klein, Ralph Lauren
1970–1980	Post-modern era	Post-modernism; Corporate modernist architecture; New Hollywood (Silver Age) – Scorsese, Coppola, blockbusters – Lucas *Star Wars*, Spielberg *Jaws*; metal, disco, reggae, punk, ska; Clash, Sex Pistols, Philip Glass; Armani, Westwood
1980–1990	Era of excess	High-tech architecture; conceptual art; Corporate Hollywood and hi-concept, Schwarzenegger, Cruise *Top Gun*; Salman Rushdie; pop, rap, hip-hop, acid house, indy, world music; Michael Jackson *Thriller*, Madonna; MTV; *Cats*; Japanese fashion (Issey Miyake, Kenzo, Rei Kawakubo), Karan (knitwear), Versace
1990–2000	Post-ironic era	Biomorphic architecture; Britart, Damien Hirst; Independent movies, Tarantino, *The Matrix*; *ER*, *Friends*, reality TV; Grunge, nu-metal; Galliano, McQueen
2000–Present	Post Millennium	Internet and web culture; Celebrity mania – OJ Simpson trial; Oprah's book club; *Harry Potter*; *Lord of the Rings* trilogy; Bollywood overtakes Hollywood in production volume; New Iranian cinema; Cultural Puritanism in Muslim states

The Seven Wonders of the Ancient World

Traditionally, the Seven Wonders of the World were the marvels of classical civilization described by Herodotus in the 5th century BCE. The list was later used and standardized by medieval writers.

Name	Date of construction	What was its fate?
Pyramids at Giza (Egypt)	c.2600–2500 BCE	The oldest of the seven wonders, and the only one to survive. For four millennia, the Great Pyramid was the world's tallest construction
Hanging Gardens of Babylon	6th century BCE	Series of terraces on the banks of the Euphrates. Built by Nebuchadnezzar II
Temple of Artemis at Ephesus, Asia Minor (now Turkey)	6th century BCE	Marble temple in honor of the goddess of hunting and the moon. Rebuilt in 4th century BCE but destroyed by Goths in 3rd century CE. A solitary column has been reerected
Statue of Zeus at Olympia	5th century BCE	30 ft-high wooden statue of Greek god Zeus covered with gold and ivory. Designed by the Athenian sculptor Phidias. Destroyed by fire in 475 CE
Mausoleum at Halicarnassus, Asia Minor (now Bodrum, Turkey)	4th century BCE	Tomb of Mausolus built by his widow. Destroyed by an earthquake before the 15th century
Colossus of Rhodes	305–292 BCE	105 ft-high bronze statue of the sun god Helios. Stood for less than a century. Destroyed by an earthquake in 224 BCE
Pharos of Alexandria	270 BCE	The world's first-known lighthouse at the entrance of Alexandria harbor in Egypt. 400 ft high. In ruins by the 15th century CE

FACT! The first mention of the Seven Wonders is in the History of Herodotus (5th century BCE), and the fact that there was a list was subsequently mentioned by other Greek writers, including Callimachus of Cyrene (305 BCE–240 BCE), Chief Librarian of the Great Library of Alexandria.

The canonical list ignores wonders of the Ancient World that belonged to other cultures, or different periods, or that the Ancient Greek and Roman writers simply hadn't seen for themselves. A more global perspective might add the following sites to the list:

Abu Simbel Temple in Egypt
Angkor Wat in Cambodia
The Aztec Temple in Tenochtitlan (Mexico City), Mexico
The Banaue Rice Terraces in the Philippines
Borobudur Temple in Indonesia
The Coliseum in Rome, Italy
The Great Wall of China
The Inca city of Machu Picchu, Peru
The Mayan Temples of Tikal in Northern Guatemala
The Moai Statues in Rapa Nui (Easter Island), Chile
The Throne Hall of Persepolis in Iran
The Parthenon in Athens, Greece
Petra, the rock-carved city in Jordan
The Shwedagon Pagoda in Myanmar
Stonehenge in England
The Taj Mahal in Agra, India
The Temple of the Inscriptions in Palenque, Mexico

The Seven Wonders of the Industrial Age
According to BBC radio, the seven great engineering feats of the Industrial era were: the SS *Great Eastern*; the Transcontinental Railway; the London Sewers; the Bell Rock Lighthouse; Brooklyn Bridge; the Panama Canal; and the Hoover Dam.

The Seven Wonders of the Modern World
According to the American Society of Civil Engineers, the greatest civil engineering works of all time are: the Empire State building; the Itaipú Dam (Brazil/Paraguay); the CN Tower; the Panama Canal; the Channel Tunnel; the North Sea Protection Works (comprising the Zuider Zee Dam and the Oosterschelde Barrier in the Netherlands); and the Golden Gate Bridge.

Great Inventions

Most of the inventions listed here have been included for the significance of their impact on society and science—with the possible exception of the safety pin, the "inventor's invention."

What?	When?	Where?	Who?
Bronze	c.3500 BCE	Fertile Crescent, Middle East	Sumerians
Wheel	c.3500 BCE	Fertile Crescent	Sumerians
Writing	c.3000 BCE	Fertile Crescent	Sumerians
Abacus	c.3000 BCE	Fertile Crescent	Babylonians
Central heating/ civilization	c.2500 BCE	Indus Valley	Mohenjo-Daro
Plumbing/Iron	c.2000 BCE	Turkey	Hittites
Glass	c.2000 BCE	Egypt	Egyptians
Moveable type	c.1500 BCE	China	Chinese
Mechanical clock	1090 BCE	China	Su Sung
Compass	c.100 BCE (possibly much earlier)	China	Jade collectors of Cheng
Paper	105 CE	China	Ts'ai Lun
Printing press	1430s	Germany	Johann Gutenberg
Microscope	1590	Netherlands	Hans Jannsen
Telescope (refracting)	1608 (first recorded patent)	Netherlands	Hans Lippershey
Calculator (mechanical)	1642 (first working model)	France	Blaise Pascal
Steam engine	1712	Britain	Thomas Newcomen
Spinning Jenny	1764	Britain	James Hargreaves
Vaccination (smallpox)	1796	Britain	Edward Jenner
Hot-air balloon	1783	France	Joseph and Etienne Montgolfier
Railway engine	1814	Britain	George Stephenson
Photography	1826	France	Joseph Niepce

What?	When?	Where?	Who?
Dynamo	1831	Britain	Michael Faraday
Computer	1833	Britain	Charles Babbage
Telegraph (electric)	1837	US/Britain	Samuel Morse/ Charles Wheatstone
Safety pin	1849	US	Walter Hunt
Dynamite	1866	Sweden	Alfred Nobel
Telephone	1876	US	Alexander Graham Bell
Light bulb	1878	Britain	Joseph Swann
Motion picture camera	1891	US	Thomas Edison
Radio telegraphy	1894	Italy	Guglielmo Marconi
Aeroplane	1903	US	Orville and Wilbur Wright
Jet engine	1930	Britain	Frank Whittle
Television (electronic)	1930	US	Vladimir Zworykin
Nylon	1935	US	W. Carothers et al
Mobile phone	1938	US	Al Gross
Microprocessor	1969	US	Ted Hoff
Internet (ARPAnet)	1969	US	Department of Defense
PC (the Altair)	1974	US	Micro Instrumentation Telemetry Systems
Buckyballs (a.k.a. fullerenes; a new form of carbon)	1985	US and UK	Robert Curl Jr, Harold Kroto, Richard Smalley
High-temperature superconductors	1986	Switzerland	Georg Bednorz and Alex Müller
Clockwork radio	1991	UK	Trevor Baylis
Robotic vacuum cleaner	2002	US	iRobot
Nanomotor (atomic-scale electric motor)	2003	US	Alex Zettl and Adam Fennimore

Speed records

Land

Land-speed record: *763.04 mph over one mile; by Andy Green (UK)
in* Thrust SSC; *at Black Rock Desert, Nevada; on October 15, 1997.*

Land-speed record for motorbikes: *322.15 mph; by Dave Campos
(US) on* Easyriders; *at Bonneville Salt Flats, Utah; on July 14, 1990.*

World's fastest and most powerful production car: *McLaren F1.
Develops 627 bhp and has recorded a top speed of 240 mph—still the
official fastest speed by a production car, even though it debuted in 1993.
This is partly because newer cars, such as the Ferrari Enzo, which are
probably faster, have not yet been officially recorded as faster.*

Fastest acceleration: *0–100 mph in under 0.5 seconds; by Sammy
"Slammin" Miller in the rocket-powered drag racer* Vanishing Point.

Fastest rail vehicle: *unmanned rocket sled, US; 6,400 mph—Mach
8.6—on April 30, 2003.*

Water

Water-speed record: *317.6 mph; by Ken Warby (Aus) in* Spirit of
Australia; *at Blowering Dam, New South Wales, Australia; on October
8, 1978.*

Air

Fastest rocket-powered aircraft: *experimental rocket ship X-15-2–
Mach 6.72 (4,554 mph) during a dive from high altitude in 1968.*

Fastest passenger aircraft: *the record was held by Concorde—top speed
of Mach 2.2 (1,450 mph). The airplane made its last flight in 2003.*

FACT! Water-speed record chasing is probably the most
dangerous sport in the world. Of the last three men to hold
the record, two died in speedboat accidents.

GENERAL
REFERENCE

Squares, Cubes, and Roots

For roots, locate your number in the appropriate column and read back to first (far-left) column. For example, to find the cube root of 343, locate this figure in the column for 3rd power, then read back to the left-hand column. Answer = 7.

Number	2nd power (squares)	3rd power (cubes)	4th power	5th power	6th power	7th power
2	4	8	16	32	64	128
3	9	27	81	243	729	2,187
4	16	64	256	1,024	4,096	16,384
5	25	125	625	3,125	15,625	78,125
6	36	216	1,296	7,776	46,656	279,936
7	49	343	2,401	16,807	117,649	823,543
8	64	512	4,096	32,768	262,144	2,097,152
9	81	729	6,561	59,049	531,441	4,782,969
10	100	1,000	10,000	100,000	1,000,000	10,000,000
11	121	1,331	14,641	161,051	1,771,561	19,487,171
12	144	1,728	20,736	248,832	2,985,984	35,831,808

FACT! Pi (π) is a potentially infinite number which is equal to the circumference divided by the diameter of any circle. Here it is calculated to 100 decimal places:

3.1415926535 8979323846 2643383279
5028841971 6939937510 5820974944
5923078164 0628620899 8628034825
3421170679

Basic geometrical formulae

Areas

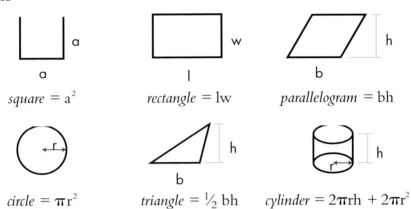

$square = a^2$

$rectangle = lw$

$parallelogram = bh$

$circle = \pi r^2$

$triangle = \frac{1}{2} bh$

$cylinder = 2\pi rh + 2\pi r^2$

Volumes

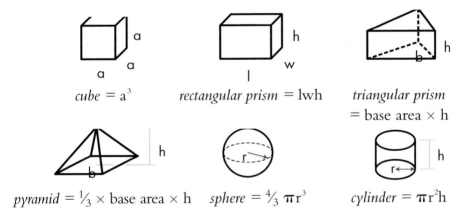

$cube = a^3$

$rectangular\ prism = lwh$

$triangular\ prism$
$= base\ area \times h$

$pyramid = \frac{1}{3} \times base\ area \times h$

$sphere = \frac{4}{3} \pi r^3$

$cylinder = \pi r^2 h$

Surface Area

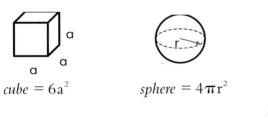

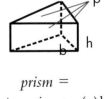

$cube = 6a^2$

$sphere = 4\pi r^2$

$prism =$
$2b + perimeter(p)h$

The International System of Units

Quantitative measurement is the cornerstone of modern science. Systems of weights and measures were developed on an *ad hoc* basis since the beginning of recorded history, but the International System of Units, or *Systeme Internationale* (SI), is an improved and unified metric system adopted by the Eleventh General Conference of Weights and Measures in 1960. It is the universal measuring system used in all areas of science throughout the world.

Names of Large Numbers

Number of zeros	SI terminology	Number of zeros	SI terminology	Number of zeros	SI terminology	Number of zeros	SI terminology
3	Thousand	21	Sextillion	39	Duodecillion	57	Octodecillion
6	Million	24	Septillion	42	Tredecillion	60	Novemdecillion
9	Billion	27	Octillion	45	Quattuordecillion	100	Googol
12	Trillion	30	Nonillion	48	Quindecillion	Googol	Googolplex
15	Quadrillion	33	Decillion	51	Sexdecillion		
18	Quintillion	36	Undecillion	54	Septendecillion		

SI Base Units

The entire SI system of measurement is constructed from seven base units, each of which represents a single physical quantity as shown in the table below.

Base quantity	Name	Symbol	Base quantity	Name	Symbol
length	meter	m	thermodynamic temperature	kelvin	K
mass	kilogram	kg	amount of substance	mole	mol
time	second	s	luminous intensity	candela	cd
electric current	ampere	A			

Temperature Conversion

In the 1700s, G. Daniel Fahrenheit developed a scale used by meteorologists for measuring surface temperature. The unit of measure is degree Fahrenheit (F°). In the same century, a second scale was developed with the unit of measure degree Celsius (C°). A third scale later developed for use by scientists became known as the Kelvin scale.

Fahrenheit shows 212° for boiling point and 32° for freezing. Celsius shows 100° for boiling point and 0° for ice. The Kelvin scale begins at absolute zero, the lowest temperature believed possible. The United States primarily uses the Fahrenheit scale; the rest of the world uses Celsius, and scientists use either the Celsius or Kelvin scale. To convert from one scale to another use the formulae:

$$°C = (°F - 32) \times \tfrac{5}{9}$$
$$°F = (°C \times \tfrac{9}{5}) + 32$$
$$K = °C + 273$$

Thermometer Markings

Kelvin (K) "Absolute"	Celsius (°C)	Fahrenheit (°F)	Kelvin (K) "Absolute"	Celsius (°C)	Fahrenheit (°F)	Kelvin (K) "Absolute"	Celsius (°C)	Fahrenheit (°F)
0	−273.15	−459.67	255.372	−17.77	0	323.15	50	122
73.15	−200	−328	273.15	0	32	328.15	55	131
93.15	−180	−292	278.15	5	41	333.15	60	140
113.15	−160	−256	283.15	10	50	338.15	65	149
133.15	−140	−220	288.15	15	59	343.15	70	158
153.15	−120	−184	293.15	20	68	348.15	75	167
173.15	−100	−148	298.15	25	77	353.15	80	176
193.15	−80	−112	303.15	30	86	358.15	85	185
213.15	−60	−76	308.15	35	95	363.15	90	194
233.15	−40	−40	313.15	40	104	368.15	95	203
253.15	−20	−4	318.15	45	113	373.15	100	212

Weights and Measures

Length

imperial >		metric
1 inch (in)		2.54 cm
1 foot (ft)	12 in	0.3048 m
1 yard (yd)	3 ft	0.9144 m
1 mile	1760 yd	1.6093 km
1 int nautical mile	2025.4 yd	1.853 km

metric >		imperial
1 millimeter (mm)		0.03937 in
1 centimeter (cm)	10 mm	0.3937 in
1 meter (m)	100 cm	1.0936 yd
1 kilometer (km)	1000 m	0.6214 mile

Area

metric >		imperial
1 sq inch (in^2)		6.4516 cm^2
1 sq foot (ft^2)	144 in^2	0.0929 m^2
1 sq yd (yd^2)	9 ft^2	0.8361 m^2
1 acre	4840 yd^2	4046.9 m^2
1 sq mile (mile^2)	640 acres	2.59 km^2

metric >		imperial
1 sq cm (cm^2)	100 mm^2	0.1550 in^2
1 sq m (m^2)	10,000 cm^2	1.1960 yd^2
1 hectare (ha)	10,000 m^2	2.4711 acres
1 sq km (km^2)	100 ha	0.3861 mile^2

Volume/Capacity

metric >		imperial
1 cu inch (in^3)		16.387 cm^3
1 cu foot (ft^3)	1,728 in^3	0.0283 m^3
1 fluid ounce (fl oz)		28.413 ml
1 pint (pt)	20 fl oz	0.5683 l
1 gallon (gal)	8 pt	4.5461 l

metric >		imperial
1 cu cm (cm^3)		0.0610 in^3
1 cu decimeter (dm^3)	1,000 cm^3	0.0353 ft^3
1 cu meter (m^3)	1,000 dm^3	1.3080 yd^3
1 liter (l)	1 dm^3	1.76 pt
1 hectoliter (hl)	100 l	21.997 gal

imperial (US)	Imperial (UK)	metric
1 fluid ounce	1.0408 fl oz	29.574 ml
1 pint (16 fl oz)	0.8327 pt	0.4731 l
1 gallon	0.8327 gal	3.7854 l

Mass

imperial >		metric		metric >		imperial
1 ounce (oz)	437.5 grain	28.35 g		1 milligram (mg)		0.0154 grain
1 pound (lb)	16 oz	0.4536 kg		1 gram (g)	1,000 mg	0.0353 oz
1 stone	14 lb	6.3503 kg		1 kilogram (kg)	1,000 g	2.2046 lb
1 hundredweight (cwt)	112 lb	50.802 kg		1 tonne (t)	1,000 kg	0.9842 ton
1 long ton (UK)	20 cwt	1.016 t				

Measures of Time

Lunar Month	Weeks	Day	Hours	Minutes	Seconds
				1	60
			1	60	3,600
		1	24	1,440	86,400
	1	7	168	10,080	604,800
1	4	28	672	40,320	2,419,200

Mean Sidereal Day

The period of time during which the Earth makes one revolution on its axis relative to a particular star—23h 56m 4.09s.

Mean Solar Day

The period of time during which the Earth makes on revolution its axis relative to the Sun—24h 0m 0.59s.

The Year

The Earth revolves around the Sun in 365 days, 5 hours, 48 minutes and 45 seconds. A calendar year is therefore usually 365 days. Leap years deal with the accumulation of the surplus time.

Leap Year

Leap years are those years divisible by 4 without a remainder. However, a century year must be divisible by 400 without a remainder (like 2000) in order to be a leap year.

Proof System for Alcohol

The US and UK proof systems hark back to an era when measuring the alcohol content of a drink was harder than today, owing to the lack of technology. Since then, the US system has been standardized to fall into line with a system of alcohol percentage by volume, where 100 proof spirit is defined as a spirit that is 50 percent alcohol by volume (and pure alcohol is 200 proof). So to convert the US proof measurement into a measurement of alcohol by volume you simply halve it. The British (Sikes) system is much more complicated and has accordingly been superceded by the Gay Lussac system that measures alcohol content by volume and is written on the side of bottles as, e.g., 40° (which means 40 percent alcohol by volume).

Percentage (a.k.a. Gay-Lussac system)	US Proof system	British Proof system (Sikes)
100 (pure alcohol)	200	175
77.5	155	135.6
75	150	131.3
60	120	105
57.14	114.29	100 (proof)
52.5	105	91.9
50	100 (proof)	87.5
48	96	84
45	90	78.7
43	86	75.2
40	80	70
37.1	74.3	65
28.6	57.1	50
22.9	45.7	40
0 (water)	0 (water)	0 (water)

FACT! The term "proof" for alcohol dates back to the 17th century. People needed a way to tell if the spirit they were buying had the right alcohol content. This was achieved by mixing the spirit with gunpowder. If its alcohol content was high enough, the powder would still ignite and the spirit was said to have been "proved"—i.e. there was proof that it contained enough alcohol to allow gunpowder to ignite. If the spirit-powder mix did not simply flare but actually exploded, the spirit was said to be "over-proof."

Big Mac Economic Indicator

The Big Mac index was devised by the *Economist* magazine as a measure of "purchasing power parity"—what can be bought in different places for the same amount of money (where the money is US dollars—the basic unit of the international economy). This makes a better way of comparing local prices than simply converting currencies according to their official exchange rates, and it also gives an excellent measure of whether or not a currency is over or undervalued in relation to the US dollar.

The index uses the price of a Big Mac hamburger because it is an everyday commodity that is made to almost exactly the same recipe in 118 countries around the world. The local price of a Big Mac is converted into US dollars, according to the current exchange rate, and can then be compared to the price of a Big Mac in the US.

National Currencies

Country	Currency	Code	Symbol
Argentina	Argentine Peso	ARS	$
Australia	Australian Dollar	AUD	A$
Austria	Euro	EUR	€
Bangladesh	Taka	BDT	Tk
Belgium	Euro	EUR	€
Brazil	Brazilian Real	BRL	R$
Canada	Canadian Dollar	CAD	Can$
China	Yuan Renminbi	CNY	¥
Cuba	Cuban Peso	CUP	Cu$
Czech Republic	Czech Koruna	CZK	Kč
Denmark	Danish Krone	DKK	Dkr
Egypt	Egyptian Pound	EGP	£E
Finland	Euro	EUR	€
France	Euro	EUR	€
Germany	Euro	EUR	€
Greece	Euro	EUR	€
Hungary	Forint	HUF	Ft
India	Indian Rupee	INR	Rs
Indonesia	Rupiah	IDR	Rp
Iran	Iranian Rial	IRR	Rls
Iraq	Iraqi Dinar	IQD	ID
Ireland	Euro	EUR	€
Israel	New Israeli Shekel	ILS	NIS
Italy	Euro	EUR	€
Japan	Yen	JPY	¥
Kenya	Kenyan Shilling	KES	K Sh
Korea (South)	Won	KRW	W

Country	Currency	Code	Symbol
Libya	Libyan Dinar	LYD	LD
Malaysia	Malaysian Ringgit	MYR	M$
Mexico	Mexican Peso	MXN	Mex$
Morocco	Moroccan Dirham	MAD	DH
Netherlands	Euro	EUR	€
New Zealand	New Zealand Dollar	NZD	NZ$
Nigeria	Naira	NGN	☐
Norway	Norwegian Krone	NOK	NKr
Pakistan	Pakistan Rupee	PKR	Rs
Philippines	Philippine Peso	PHP	☐
Poland	Zloty	PLN	Zł
Portugal	Euro	EUR	€
Russia	Russian Rouble	RUR	R
Saudi Arabia	Saudi Riyal	SAR	SRls
Singapore	Singapore Dollar	SGD	S$
South Africa	Rand	ZAR	R
Spain	Euro	EUR	€
Sweden	Swedish Krona	SEK	Sk
Switzerland	Swiss Franc	CHF	SwF
Syria	Syrian Pound	SYP	£S
Taiwan	New Taiwan Dollar	TWD	NT$
Thailand	Baht	THB	Bht or Bt
Turkey	Turkish Lira	TRL	TL
Ukraine	Hryvna	UAH	UAH
United Kingdom	Pound Sterling	GBP	£
United States	U.S. Dollar	USS	US$

The Compass

The Earth is like a huge magnet, with the lines of magnetic force running north and south. The compass was developed from the magnetic needle of the Chinese. The needle on a compass points to magnetic north, drawn by Earth's natural magnetic fields. By convention the cardinal points are measured east of north, i.e. North is 0°, East is 90°, South is 180°, and West is 270°.

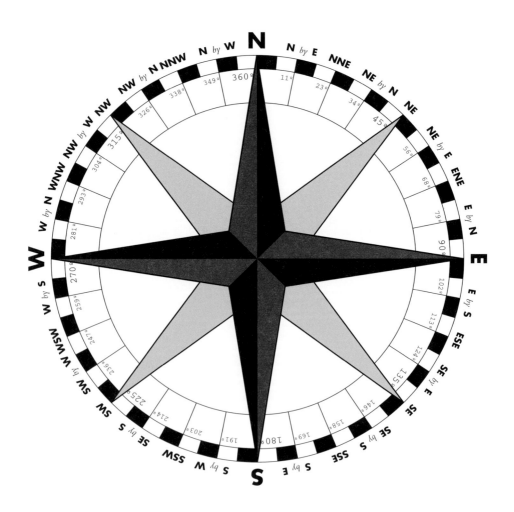

Magnetic North and True North

The North Pole, the most northerly geographical point on the planet, and magnetic north (the north to which the compass needle points) are two different locations. The difference is known as declination, or magnetic variation. Navigators have to apply a correction to their compass readings so that their bearings can be transferred to their charts. Because the position of magnetic north is slowly shifting, the variation in a given area changes from year to year.

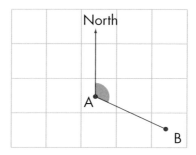

All navigational maps note the magnetic variation in numbers of degrees for that area in a key, together with the rate of change. It is necessary to know the magnetic variation when navigating in order to change a map bearing (the angle between the line of your course and North) into an accurate magnetic bearing.

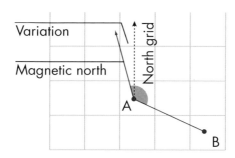

To make the correction, when the magnetic variation is west of North you turn the compass anticlockwise to add the required number of degrees.

When the magnetic variation is east of North, turn the compass clockwise to deduct the number of degrees of the magnetic variation.

Flags and Codes

The Morse Code

This internationally recognized code is composed of dots and dashes that represent letters and numerals. It was invented in 1838 by Samuel F. B. Morse who was also the inventor of the telegraph. The dash is three times the length of a dot. A space the length of a dot is left between symbols, two dots between letters and a dash between words.

Here is the complete Morse code:

A	•—	J	•———	S	•••	1	•————
B	—•••	K	—•—	T	—	2	••———
C	—•—•	L	•—••	U	••—	3	•••——
D	—••	M	——	V	•••—	4	••••—
E	•	N	—•	W	•——	5	•••••
F	••—•	O	———	X	—••—	6	—••••
G	——•	P	•——•	Y	—•——	7	——•••
H	••••	Q	——•—	Z	——••	8	———••
I	••	R	•—•	0	—————	9	————•

The Semaphore Code

Favored by Girl and Boy Scouts troops, the Semaphore code uses hand-held flags (or lights) to signal messages between two people within sight of each other. Developed by the Frenchman Claude Chappe in 1794 using pivoted arms on a post, the relative positions of the two flags denote letters of the alphabet and numerals.

The transmission begins with the letters V.O.X. or V.E. being signaled, or the International Code flag J being hoisted. The signaller then awaits a go-ahead signal back from the receiver before continuing.

The Semaphore alphabet is shown opposite:

Radio Lingo and International Flag Codes

Letter	Radio lingo	Flag	Meaning
A	Alpha		Diver below/I am undergoing speed trials
B	Bravo		I am loading/discharging explosives
C	Charlie		Affirmative
D	Delta		Keep clear/I am manuevering with difficulty
E	Echo		I am altering course to starboard
F	Foxtrot		I am disabled, communicate with me
G	Golf		I require a pilot
H	Hotel		I have a pilot onboard
I	India		I am altering course to port
J	Juliet		I am going to send a message by Semaphore
K	Kilo		Stop your vessel immediately
L	Lima		Stop immediately, I need to communicate
M	Mike		I have a doctor onboard
N	November		Negative
O	Oscar		Man overboard
P	Papa		Vessel about to depart/your lights are out
Q	Quebec		My vessel is healthy
R	Romeo		My way is off, You may pass me slowly
S	Sierra		My engines are full astern
T	Tango		Do not pass ahead of me
U	Uniform		You are standing into danger
V	Victor		I require assistance
W	Whisky		I require medical assistance
X	X-ray		Stop your movements and watch for my signals
Y	Yankee		I carry mail
Z	Zulu		To call or address shore stations

Emergency Signals

At Sea
The following signals indicate an emergency at sea and a request for help:

1. *A parachute flare or hand flare showing a red light.*
2. *Rockets that throw off red stars at intervals.*
3. *Smoke signals giving off large volumes of orange smoke.*
4. *Signal by radio in the Morse Code group SOS or the spoken word MAYDAY (do not use this except in life-threatening emergencies).*
5. *Slowly raising and lowering your arms repeatedly.*
6. *Continuous sounding of whistle or siren (as contrasted to the ground signal in groups of 3).*
7. *Flames on the vessel (i.e. from the burning of an oily rag).*
8. *Flying the International Flag code signal NC (if you have it).*
9. *Flying a square flag with a ball (or something resembling a ball) above or below it.*
10. *An ensign (flag) flown upside down.*
11. *A coat or article of clothing on an oar or mast.*

When Hiking
If you run into trouble while hiking or in any other situation on land, the following signals indicate a request for help:

1. *A triangle—made out of three fires or reflective/visible material.*
2. *Recognized signals spelt out in sticks on the ground are:*
    SOS or HELP (general need for help)
    I – Someone is injured.
    X – Unable to proceed.
    F – Need food and water.
3. *A flashing mirror—flash in groups of three.*
4. *Whistle blasts—in groups of three.*
5. *Loud banging in groups of three—bang together rocks or sticks.*

Emoticons

The following symbols and abbreviations are used in cellphone text messaging and emails:

Emoticon	English	Emoticon	English
:-)	happy	**S/o**	someone
:-))	very happy	**RUOK**	Are you okay?
:-(	sad	**RUBZ**	Are you busy?
:-((	very sad	**Thx**	Thanks
:'-(	crying	**CUL8R**	See you later
:-*	kiss	**IMS**	I am sorry
;-)	wink	**ILUVU**	I love you
:-O	wow!	**PLS**	Please
:-x	not saying a word	**XLNT**	Excellent

International Sign Language

Each country has its own sign language. In an attempt to devise a universal sign language—a sort of sign equivalent to the universal spoken and written language Esperanto—the World Federation of the Deaf first proposed the idea of creating an International Sign Language (ISL) in 1951, when it was tentatively named Gestuno. Work began in 1973. Over the years, ISL evolved by borrowing gestures from national sign languages.

ISL is limited, has no proper grammar, and is only widely used at international conferences or the Deaflympics. More universal is the American Sign Language finger-spelling alphabet, which allows a signer to spell out words letter by letter.

Finger-spelling Alphabet

A	J	S	2
B	K	T	3
C	L	U	4
D	M	V	5
E	N	W	6
F	O	X	7
G	P	Y	8
H	Q	Z	9
I	R	1	0

Common Latin Phrases

a priori from what was before

ad absurdum to the point of absurdity

ad hoc for this special purpose

ad hominem appealing to feelings rather than reason

ad infinitum without limit

ad nauseam to a tedious extent

addenda items to be added

affidavit a sworn written statement usable as evidence in court

alma mater old school or college

alter ego other self

annus horribilis a bad year

annus mirabilis a wonderful year

ante bellum before the war

ars gratia artis art for art's sake

bona fide (adjective) genuine

carpe diem seize the day

casus belli the circumstances justifying war

caveat emptor let the buyer beware

circa (abbreviated c and followed by a date) about

cogito, ergo sum I think, therefore I am (Descartes)

compos mentis sane

cui bono? who benefits?

curriculum vitae a summary of a person's career

de facto in fact (especially in contradistinction to *de jure*)

de jure by right (especially in contradistinction to *de facto*)

deus ex machina a contrived event that resolves a problem at the last moment

dramatis personae the list of characters in a play

ecce homo behold the man

ego consciousness of one's own identity

ergo therefore

et alii (abbreviated *et al*) and others

ex cathedra (of a pronouncement) formally, with official authority

fiat let it be done

habeas corpus you may have the body. (The opening words of a prerogative writ requiring a person holding another person to bring that person before a court.)

ibidem (abbreviated *ibid* in citations of books, etc) in the same place

in absentia while absent

in extremis near death

in flagrante delicto in the very act of committing an offence

in loco parentis in place of a parent

in memoriam in memory

in situ in its original situation

in vino veritas in wine there is truth

in vitro outside the living body and in an artificial environment

in vivo happening within a living organism

infra below or on a later page

inter alia among other things

ipso facto by that very fact

magna cum laude with great honor or distinction

magnum opus great work

mea culpa by my fault (used as an acknowledgment of error)

memento mori remember that you have to die

mens rea guilty mind

mens sana in corpore sano a sound mind in a sound body

modus operandi the manner of working

mutatis mutandis the necessary changes being made

non sequitur it does not follow

passim in various places (in a quoted work)

per annum per year

per ardua ad astra through difficulties to the stars

per capita by the head

per centum per hundred

per diem per day

per se taken alone

persona non grata a non-acceptable person

post mortem after death (also figuratively)

prima facie on a first view

pro bono done without charge in the public interest

pro forma for the sake of form

pro rata according to the rate

pro tempore (abbreviated *pro tem*) for the time being

quid pro quo something for something

quo vadis? where are you going?

quod erat demonstrandum (abbreviated QED) which was to be proved

quod vide (abbreviated *q.v.*) which see

reductio ad absurdum reduction to the absurd (proving the truth of a proposition by proving the falsity of all its alternatives)

sic thus

sic transit gloria mundi thus passes the glory of the world

sine qua non an indispensable condition

status quo the existing condition

stet let it stand

sub judice before a court

tempus fugit time flies

terra firma dry land

terra incognita unknown land

vade mecum a constant companion

veni, vidi, vici I came, I saw, I conquered (Caesar)

verbatim exactly as said

vice versa the order being reversed

vox populi voice of the people

Roman Numerals

Roman numerals are used to denote dates on buildings, books, and clockfaces. The symbols are added together to arrive at the total value; but when a symbol of lesser value appears in front of one of higher value, that symbol is subtracted. For example, VI is V+I = 6 whereas IV is V-I = 4.

Arabic	Romam numeral	Arabic	Romam numeral
1	I	40	XL
2	II	45	VL
3	III	50	L
4	IV	80	XXC
5	V	90	XC
6	VI	100	C
7	VII	400	CD
8	VIII	500	D
9	IX	800	CCM
10	X	1000	M

Chinese Numerals

These symbols are for the basic numerals. For other numbers, you will have to combine them. For example, 15 is 十 五 , 25 is 二 十 五 , and 50 is 五 十 .

Number	Character	Number	Character	Number	Character
1	一	7	七	10 000	万
2	二	8	八	1 000 000 (million)	百 万
3	三	9	九		
4	四	10	十	100 000 000 (one hundred million)	亿
5	五	100	百		
6	六	1 000	千	1 000 000 000 (billion)	十 亿

The Greek Alphabet

The Greek Alphabet is used often in science, particularly mathematics. The word alphabet is itself derived from the first two Greek letters.

Capital	Lowercase	Character	Capital	Lowercase	Character	Capital	Lowercase	Character
A	α	alpha	I	ι	iota	P	ρ	rho
B	β	beta	K	κ	kappa	Σ	σ	sigma
Γ	γ	gamma	Λ	λ	lambda	T	τ	tau
Δ	δ	delta	M	μ	mu	Υ	υ	upsilon
E	ε	epsilon	N	ν	nu	Φ	φ	phi
Z	ζ	zeta	Ξ	ξ	xi	X	χ	chi
H	η	eta	O	o	omicron	Ψ	ψ	psi
Θ	θ	theta	Π	π	pi	Ω	ω	omega

Greek Numerals

	Units	Tens	Hundreds
1	A (alpha)	I (iota)	P (rho)
2	B (beta)	K (kappa)	Σ (sigma)
3	Γ (gamma)	Λ (lambda)	T (tau)
4	Δ (delta)	M (mu)	Θ (upsilon)
5	E (epsilon)	N (nu)	Φ (phi)
6	ϛ (digamma)	X (xi)	Ψ (chi)
7	Z (zeta)	O (omicron)	Υ (psi)
8	H (eta)	Π (pi)	ϐ (omega)
9	Θ (theta)	Ϙ (koppa)	⊤ or ⋀ (sampi)

New Year Around the World

Chinese New Year

The date of the Chinese New Year is determined by the new cycle of the Moon falling between January 21 and February 19. Each year is named for a symbolic animal, in sequential order: Rat, Ox, Tiger, Rabbit, Dragon, Snake, Horse, Goat, Monkey, Rooster, Dog, and Pig.

Hindu New Year

Diwali is a five-day Hindu festival on the 15th day of the Indian month of Kartika (in October or November). *Diwali* is a corruption of the Sanskrit *Deepavali—Deepa* meaning light and *Avali* meaning a row. Every home is lit with lamps to welcome Lakshmi, Goddess of wealth and prosperity. The fourth day of *Diwali* is looked upon as the beginning of the New Year.

Islamic New Year

The Hegirian calendar is based on the cycles of the Moon. Muharram is the first month of the Muslim year and its first day is celebrated as New Year's Day. It is observed quietly in the mosques when special prayers are said. The most important part of the new year is the telling of the story of the Flight of Medina.

Jewish New Year

Rosh Hashanah is Hebrew for "beginning of the year" and is celebrated on the first and second days of the Jewish month Tishri (in September or October). The *shofar*, a wind instrument made of ram's horn to represent the animal sacrificed in Isaac's stead, is blown during the service.

Western New Year

In the Middle Ages, the Julian calendar observed New Year's Day on March 25. The date was gradually changed to January 1 with the introduction of the Gregorian calendar in 1582. A chorus of "Auld Lang Syne" (a traditional Scottish song) is often sung at midnight.

Glossary

astrology The divination of the supposed influences of the stars and planets on human affairs and terrestrial events by their positions and aspects.

astronomy The study of objects and matter outside the earth's atmosphere and of their physical and chemical properties.

atmosphere The gaseous envelope of a celestial body (as a planet); the whole mass of air surrounding the earth.

biomass the amount of living matter (as in a unit area or volume of habitat); plant materials and animal waste used especially as a source of fuel.

biome A major ecological community type (as tropical rain forest, grassland, or desert).

climate A region of the earth having specified climatic conditions; the average course or condition of the weather at a place usually over a period of years as exhibited by temperature, wind velocity, and precipitation.

coordinate Any of a set of numbers used in specifying the location of a point on a line, on a surface, or in space; any one of a set of variables used in specifying the state of a substance or the motion of a particle or momentum.

cosmic Of or relating to the cosmos, the extraterrestrial vastness, or the universe in contrast to the earth alone; of, relating to, or concerned with abstract spiritual or metaphysical ideas; characterized by greatness especially in extent, intensity, or comprehensiveness.

density The quality or state of being compact or crowded together or of having a high mass per unit volume.

desertification The process of becoming desert (as from land mismanagement or climate change).

eccentric Deviating from a circular path; elliptical; located elsewhere than at the geometrical center.

elliptical Oval-shaped.

erosion The gradual destruction of something by natural forces (such as water, wind, or ice); the process by which something is eroded or worn away.

extrapolate To project, extend, or expand (known data or experience) into an area not known or experienced so as to arrive at a usually conjectural knowledge of the unknown area; to predict by projecting past experience or known data.

fusion The union of atomic nuclei to form heavier nuclei resulting in the release of enormous quantities of energy when certain light elements unite; a union by or as if by melting; a merging of diverse, distinct, or separate elements into a unified whole.

galaxy Any of the very large groups of stars and associated matter that are found throughout the universe.

hominid Any of a family (Hominidae) of erect bipedal primate mammals that includes recent humans together with extinct ancestral and related forms and in some recent classifications the gorilla, chimpanzee, and orangutan.

infinitesimal Immeasurably or incalculably small.

kingdom One of the three primary divisions into which natural objects are commonly classified—animal, plant, and mineral; a major category in biological taxonomy that ranks above the phylum and below the domain.

nebulae Any of numerous clouds of gas or dust in interstellar space.

pictogram An ancient or prehistoric drawing or painting on a rock wall; one of the symbols belonging to a pictorial graphic system; a diagram representing statistical data by pictorial forms.

salinity A measure of salt content; consisting of or containing salt; relating to or resembling salt.

species A class of individuals having common attributes and designated by a common name; a logical division of a genus or more comprehensive class; a category of biological classification ranking immediately below the genus or subgenus, comprising related organisms or populations potentially capable of interbreeding.

tectonics Geological structural features as a whole; a branch of geology concerned with the structure of the crust of a planet (as earth) or moon and especially with the formation of folds and faults in it.

universe The entire celestial cosmos; the milky way galaxy; an aggregate of stars comparable to the Milky Way galaxy.

For More Information

American Museum of Natural History
Central Park West at 79th Street
New York, NY 10024-5192
(212) 769-5100
Web site: http://www.amnh.org
The American Museum of Natural History is one of the world's
preeminent scientific and cultural institutions. Since its founding in
1869, the museum has advanced its global mission to discover, interpret,
and disseminate information about human cultures, the natural world
and the universe through a wide-ranging program of scientific research,
education, and exhibition. The museum is renowned for its exhibitions
and scientific collections, which serve as a field guide to the entire
planet and present a panorama of the world's cultures.

Canadian Space Agency
John H. Chapman Space Centre
6767 Route de l'Aéroport
Saint-Hubert, QC J3Y 8Y9
Canada
(450) 926-4800
Web site: http://www.asc-csa.gc.ca/eng/default.asp
Established in March 1989, the Canadian Space Agency (CSA) is
committed to leading the development and application of space
knowledge for the benefit of Canadians.

Canadian Museum of Civilization
100 Laurier Street
Gatineau, QC K1A 0M8
Canada
(800) 555-5621
Web site: http://www.civilization.ca/home
Canada's national museum of human history and the most popular
and most-visited

Johnson Space Center
1601 NASA Parkway

Houston, TX 77058
(281) 244-2100
Web site: http://www.nasa.gov/centers/johnson/home/index.html
Johnson Space Center was established in 1961, and from the early
    Gemini, Apollo, and Skylab projects to the Space Shuttle and
    International Space Station Programs and beyond into future space
    missions, the center continues to lead NASA's efforts in human
    space exploration.

Kennedy Space Center
SR 405
Kennedy Space Center, FL 32899
(866) 737-5235
Web site: http://www.kennedyspacecenter.com/
NASA's launch headquarters is the only place on Earth where you
    can tour launch areas, meet a veteran astronaut, see giant rockets,
    train in spaceflight simulators, and even view a launch.

Museum Of Anthropology
6393 N.W. Marine Drive
Vancouver, BC V6T 1Z2
Canada
(604) 822-5087
Web site: http://www.moa.ubc.ca
The Museum of Anthropology at the University of British Columbia
    is world-renowned for its collections, research, teaching, public
    programs, and community connections.

National Aeronautics and Space Administration (NASA)
Public Communications Office
NASA Headquarters, Suite 5K39
Washington, DC 20546-0001
(202) 358-0001
Web site: http://www.nasa.gov
NASA's mission is to reach for new heights and reveal the unknown
    to benefit all humankind. NASA has a robust program of space

exploration and operations, flight technology development, and scientific research.

The National Science Foundation
Directorate for Biological Sciences
4201 Wilson Boulevard
Arlington, VA 22230
(703) 292-5111
Web site: http://www.nsf.gov/dir/index.jsp?org=BIO
The Directorate for Biological Sciences supports research to advance understanding of the principles and mechanisms governing life. Research studies extend across systems that encompass biological molecules, cells, tissues, organs, organisms, populations, communities, and ecosystems up to and including the global biosphere. NSF/BIO plays a major role in support of research resources for the biological sciences including living stock centers, systematics collections, biological field stations, computerized databases including sequence databases for plants and microorganisms. NSF/BIO is also the nation's principal supporter of fundamental academic research on plant biology, environmental biology, and biodiversity.

Science Olympiad
2 Trans Am Plaza Drive, Suite 415
Oakbrook Terrace, IL 60181
(630) 792-1251
Web site: http://www.soinc.org
Science Olympiad is a national non-profit organization dedicated to improving the quality of K-12 science education, increasing male, female, and minority interest in science, creating a technologically-literate workforce, and providing recognition for outstanding achievement by both students and teachers. These goals are achieved by participating in Science Olympiad tournaments and non-competitive events, incorporating Science Olympiad into classroom curriculum, and attending teacher training institutes.

Smithsonian National Air and Space Museum
National Mall Building
Independence Ave at 6th Street, SW
Washington, DC 20560
(202) 633-2214
Web site: http://www.nasm.si.edu

The Smithsonian Institution's National Air and Space Museum maintains the largest collection of historic air and spacecraft in the world. It is also a vital center for research into the history, science, and technology of aviation and space flight, as well as planetary science and terrestrial geology and geophysics. The Museum has two display facilities. The National Mall building in Washington, D.C. has hundreds of artifacts on display including the original Wright 1903 Flyer, the Spirit of St. Louis, the Apollo 11 command module, and a lunar rock sample that visitors can touch. The Steven F. Udvar-Hazy Center displays many more artifacts including the Lockheed SR-71 *Blackbird*, Boeing B-29 Superfortress *Enola Gay* and Space Shuttle *Enterprise*.

Web sites

Due to the changing nature of Internet links, Rosen Publishing has developed an online list of Web sites related to the subject of this book. This site is updated regularly. Please use this link to access this list:

http://www.rosenlinks.com/GCM/Univ

For Further Reading

Carroll, Sean. *The Particle at the End of the Universe: How the Hunt for the Higgs Boson Leads Us to the Edge of a New World*. New York, NY: Dutton, 2012.

Cox, Brian, and Andrew Cohen. *Wonders of the Universe*. New York, NY: Harper Design, 2011.

Cox, Brian, and Jeff Forshaw. *The Quantum Universe:* (and Why Anything that Can Happen, Does). Boston, MA: Da Capo Press, 2013.

Dickinson, Terence. *Hubble's Universe: Greatest Discoveries and Latest Images*. New York, NY: Firefly Books, 2012.

Freedman, Roger A., et al. *Universe*. New York, NY: W.H. Freeman & Co., 2010.

Halpern, Paul. *Edge of the Universe: A Voyage to the Cosmic Horizon and Beyond*. Hoboken, NJ: Wiley, 2012.

Krauss. Lawrence M. *A Universe from Nothing: Why There Is Something Rather than Nothing*. New York, NY: Atria Books, 2013.

Livio, Mario. *Brilliant Blunders: From Darwin to Einstein: Colossal Mistakes by Great Scientists that Changed Our Understanding of Life and the Universe*. New York, NY: Simon & Schuster, 2013.

Rees, Martin. *Universe*. New York, NY: DK, 2012.

Seeds, Michael A., et al. *Universe: Solar System, Stars, and Galaxies*. Boston, MA: Cengage Learning, 2011.

Shubin, Neil. *The Universe Within: Discovering the Common History of Rocks, Planets, and People*. New York, NY: Pantheon, 2013.

Trefil, James. *Space Atlas: Mapping the Universe and Beyond*. Washington, DC: National Geographic, 2012.

Index

M

magma 50
magnetic field 37
magnetosphere 19
mammals 39, 86, 87
mantle 38, 40, 50
Mariana Trench 58
Mars 24, 27, 55
mass, conversion table 123
mathematical data 118–19
measurement systems 120–5
Mercator Projection 41
Mercury 23–4
meridians 41
mesosphere 44–5
Milky Way 10–11, 13, 18
Miranda 26
monera 81
Moon 20, 22, 55
moons 24, 25, 26, 27
Morse Code 130
mortality, causes of 102
mountains 54
musculo-skeletal system 90, 91
mycelial networks 84

N

nanotechnology 63
navies 76
navigation 128–9
nebulae 11
Neptune 22, 26–7
Nereid 26
nervous system 91
nuclear weapons 77
numbers, names of large 120

O

Oberon 26
oceans 58–60
oil pollution 60
oil reserves 77
Oort Cloud 18, 20
oxygen 37, 38, 59
ozone layer 37, 49, 64

P

Phobos 24
photosphere 18, 19
photosynthesis 37, 59
phytoplankton 59

planets 9, 11, 18, 22–31, 36
plankton 59
plants 81, 84–5
plate tectonics 37, 50–1
Pluto 18, 22, 27
polar ice caps 59–60
Poles 40, 64, 128–9
pollution 60, 62, 63
population 36, 62
protista 81

Q

quasars 10

R

radial inhomogeneities 26
radiogalaxies 10
Radio Lingo 132
rainfall 47
rainforests 56–7
reproductive system 93
respiratory system 90, 91
rivers 60
Roman numerals 138
roots, mathematical 118
Roswell 33, 34

S

saddhus 99
satellites 25, 31, 45
Saturn 22, 25–6, 27
Semaphore Code 130
senses 100–1
Seyfert galaxies 10
sidereal day 123
sign language 134–5
SI System 120
sleep deprivation record 99
smell, sense of 100–1
soil, 57, 62
Solar System 10, 17–34, 36
Solar Wind 19, 20, 40
space missions 28–32
species 80–1
speed records 116
spiral galaxies 10
squares, mathematical 118
stars 8, 11–16, 18
stratosphere 44–5
stunt, greatest 105

Sun 18–19, 22, 36, 59
sunspots 19

T

taiga 85
taste, sense of 100
taxa 80
temperature conversion 121
thermosphere 44–5
thymine 94, 95
Titan 25, 27
touch, sense of 101
trees 84, 85
Triton 26
tropical climates 46, 47
troposphere 44–5
tsunami 59, 64
tumo 99

U

UFOs 33–4
ultra-violet (UV) radiation 37, 64
Umbriel 26
United Nations 75
Uranus 22, 26, 27
urinary system 93

V

vegetation 56–7
Venus 24
vision, sense of 101
Volcanic Explosivity Index 52
volcanoes 50, 51–2, 63
volume
    conversion table 122
    geometrical formula 119

W

wars 62
waterfalls 61
waves 59, 64
weather 48
weights and measures 122–3
wind-chill factor 48
wonders of the world 112–13
world war, threat of 62

Z

zodiac 16